The 100 G

The Authors

Frank Schnelle writes on cinema and produces documentaries. He studied Journalism, Theater studies and German studies, worked for several film festivals and for German TV channels Sat.1 and kabel eins. He wrote and edited books on John Carpenter, Clint Eastwood, David Fincher and BLADE RUNNER, among others. (www.schnelle-medienproduktion.de)

Andreas Thiemann holds a master degree in American Studies, Journalism and History. From 1997 to 2009, he worked for the PR department of German TV station Sat.1. Currently, he works for the marketing division of German news channel N24. He is also the co-author of *The 50 Greatest Horror Movies of All Time* and contributed to the book *David Fincher*. (www.thiemann-text.de)

Frank Schnelle / Andreas Thiemann

The
100 Greatest
Movies of All Time

The List to End All Lists

BERTZ+FISCHER

Bibliografische Information der Deutschen Nationalbibliothek
Die Deutsche Nationalbibliothek verzeichnet diese
Publikation in der Deutschen Nationalbibliografie;
detaillierte bibliografische Daten sind im Internet über
http://dnb.d-nb.de abrufbar.

Cover designed by D.B. Berlin

Photo credits:
Deutsche Kinemathek – Museum für Film und Fernsehen,
Video, DVD, and Blu-ray prints
© Photos: original copyright holders

Second Edition, 2015
© 2014 by Bertz + Fischer GbR
Wrangelstr. 67, 10997 Berlin, Germany
Printed in Poland
ISBN 978-3-86505-233-9

Contents

Introduction 6

The 100 Greatest Movies (chronological order) ... 11

Charts
Top 100: The Ranking 112
Top 100 Directors 116
Sources 120

Introduction

In order to avoid any misunderstandings, let us begin
by saying that this book does *not* present the 100 movies that we, the authors, consider to be the greatest of all
time. What we have tried to achieve in compiling this list
is something entirely different, something that has not
been done before, at least, not on this scale. Our goal was
to determine film history's definitive crème de la crème,
the titles considered to be the best not only across nation-
al borders and different media, but also across different
camps and crowds. To produce a ranking that is as im-
partial and objective as possible, we collected, combined
and, in the end, condensed all of the available lists that
have been published within the last ten years—expert
queries, audience votings, readers' polls and other rankings from magazines, institutes and websites—into one
meta-list. We believe that our »list to end all lists« estab-
lishes, more than any of the singular lists it incorporates,
the one hundred films that truly deserve to be called the
greatest of all time.

Most existing lists have their weaknesses. There are
critics' lists that tolerate neither comedies nor blockbusters. There are audience lists that champion current
mainstream fare and ignore older productions altogether;
»politically correct« lists that try to spread their selection
evenly over continents and decades; counter-lists that
campaign for overlooked and offbeat gems, and so on.
The basic idea behind our work is that, taken together,
all these lists must yield a more serious and realistic pro-
file of the very films that represent cinema's outstand-

ing productions in the eyes of experts *and* fans alike, the favorites we all agree on, be it wittingly or unwittingly, at least in our Western cultural sphere (this limitation must be emphasized).

We exclusively evaluated and analyzed sources from the last ten years, among them, film journals such as *Sight and Sound* and *Cahiers du Cinéma*, magazines such as *Esquire* and *Time*, daily newspapers such as *The Times* and the *Süddeutsche Zeitung*, television channels such as *Channel 4* and *ABC TV*, websites such as *imdb. com*, *totalfilm.com* and *filmcritic.com* as well as professional journals, TV guides and the publications of film institutes. We focused, in particular, on Anglo-American and German media, but also included French, Italian, Brazilian and Australian rankings. Of course, we cannot claim scientific exactness. After all, the original lists have been compiled by using many different criteria: some are sorted alphabetically, others by score; some consist of fewer or more than 100 titles; some aggregate the opinions of tens of thousands of participants, others rely on one person's verdict.

We have been asked why we didn't take older lists into account. The answer is simple: it would have been unfair on more recent productions which could not have entered these older lists. Also, our aim was to determine the *contemporary* taste in movies. The status of a movie changes over the years and decades; many films regarded today as undisputed milestones initially received negative reviews or were ignored by the public. It was only later that their true significance was acknowledged. Other pictures suffered a reverse fate.

We disregarded box-office results, movie awards or annual »movies of the year« lists for our ranking. All of these details can provide indications of the quality of a movie, but not much more. Whether or not a film performs strongly at the box office doesn't mean much in our context. To a degree, the same holds true for awards: their criteria are often questionable, and such merits are hard to compare between different years. Rankings dedicated to the whole of film history inevitably have greater relevance.

Our scoring system was simple: all top 100 titles of each list received the same number of points, regardless of their position on that list. Lists of major media were weighted slightly stronger. So, each mention in one of the lists pushed a film to a higher position in our overall ranking. The final results are staggering in more than one way. Barely more than 1,800 titles were mentioned at all—a remarkably low number considering the hundreds of thousands of existing productions. Only a good half of those 1,800 could claim more than two mentions for themselves. And a mere 400 titles managed to amass a significant number of multiple mentions. About 80 titles secured their place in this book early on, only the rankings between 80 and 120 were fiercely contested until the last moment. In other words, the »tip of the movie iceberg« is strikingly small, or formulated vice versa, there is a surprising consensus about the question of which films are the outstanding works of their kind.

The print version of this book presents the films chronologically instead of in ranking order. Next to the credits, you will nevertheless find their respective list position. This way, our book offers a pleasant journey through cinema history. Although we personally miss certain directors and do not claim to present an objective film canon, but rather the result of an intriguing game for cineastes, our readers can rely on these 100 titles. Be it as a starting point for excited controversial debates, as guidance in the search for movie milestones, or simply as a reliable companion for guaranteed first-rate entertainment.

Frank Schnelle and Andreas Thiemann
Berlin, January 2014

The 100 Greatest Movies (chronological order)

THE GOLD RUSH

The most beloved of all tramp stories features both the famous shoe dinner and the dancing rolls. During the gold rush of 1898, gruff prospectors, hard-boiled racketeers and naïve dreamers tried to make their fortunes in the frozen wilderness between Klondike and Yukon. Many thousands went looking for gold, but most of them found only extreme cold, blizzards, hunger, and other deprivations. A grim setting

that proves to be the perfect backdrop for Chaplin's favorite character, the little guy, and his Sisyphus-like struggle against adverse circumstances. With nothing to show but courage and endurance, a talent for improvisation and a healthy sense of humor, he defies danger and braves all storms, finds a rough-and-ready friend and, with him, a mountain of gold. Finally, he even wins the heart of his inamorata. In his inimitable way, Chaplin blends pratfalls and pathos, slapstick and melancholia into one of the greatest works of the silent era. Of all his movies, THE GOLD RUSH was his personal favorite.

The Gold Rush; USA 1925/1942; D, P, Sc: Charles Chaplin; DoP: Roland Totheroh; Cast: Charles Chaplin, Georgia Hale, Mack Swain, Tom Murray, Henry Bergman; B&W, 96 min. (1925, at 18 fps) / 72 min. (1942).

Rank
81

BATTLESHIP POTEMKIN

One of the most highly praised and influential works of art of the past century. As wild and vehement as the waves crashing against Russian shores in the opening sequence, filled to the brim with powerful images and emotionally rousing music and pregnant with symbolic meaning, POTEMKIN remains a proud battleship in the ocean of film history and mandatory viewing for anyone seriously interested in movies. Commissioned by the Central Committee to shoot

a propaganda film on the occasion of the 20th anniversary of the failed revolution of 1905, Eisenstein chose a true incident. The mutiny of sailors on the Potemkin against czarist officers is his starting point for a tragedy told in five acts. The events dramatically culminate in a massacre caused by government troops shooting into a crowd of people on the stairs to Odessa's harbor, including the oft-cited scene of an infant in a stroller precariously bouncing down the stairs. With tremendous efficacy, Eisenstein puts his complex theory of montage into practice, demonstrating, even more than the power of the people, the power of cinema.

Bronenosets Potemkin; USSR 1925; D: Sergei M. Eisenstein; P: Jacob Bliokh; Sc: Nina Agadzhanova; DoP: Vladimir Popov, Eduard Tisse; Cast: Aleksandr Antonov, Vladimir Barsky, Grigori Aleksandrov, Ivan Bobrov, Mikhail Gomorov; B&W, 75 min. / 72 min. (Blu-ray).

Rank
52

THE GENERAL

THE GENERAL might be called the blockbuster of the silent era, a film full of spectacular crowd scenes, breakneck stunts, breathtaking camera moves—and a simply ingenious, ingeniously simple plot. Stoneface Buster Keaton plays a train engineer who loves two things: his traction engine »General« and his girl Annabelle (Marion Mack). When, during the turmoil of the Civil War, he loses both, it's the beginning of a hot pursuit that involves a crazy train race and the collapse of a (real) railway bridge. Keaton and his screenwriting and directing partner Clyde Bruckman are not after slapstick in the general sense. Rather, they develop humor out of their

characters' idiosyncrasies and the story's implications. Thanks to his graveness, Keaton, unlike Chaplin, from a present-day perspective, comes across as a »modern visitor to the world of silent era clowns« (Roger Ebert).

The General; USA 1927; D, Sc: Buster Keaton, Clyde Bruckman; P: Buster Keaton, Joseph M. Schenck; DoP: Bert Haines, Dev Jennings; Cast: Buster Keaton, Marion Mack, Glen Cavender, Jim Farley, Frederick Vroom; B&W, 105 min.

14

METROPOLIS

METROPOLIS inspired the urban worlds and human machines of BLADE RUNNER and THE FIFTH ELEMENT; Fritz Lang's expressionistic vision of a divided society in which

the rich and beautiful live a life of luxury while the poor and powerless work themselves to death in gigantic factories, is the first great work of science fiction cinema. Its plot—the love between a man from above and a woman from below unites the opposites—is rather simple. Instead, Lang focuses on a musical, almost abstract direction of movement and space, on an architecture that even today leaves us speechless, on the virtuoso »ballet« of the army of extras. According to some sources, METROPOLIS was 210 minutes long at its German premiere, others speak of 153 min-

utes. That version was never released; the following editions, no matter how shortened, re-edited or »reconstructed«, were nothing else but approximations to Lang's initial vision.

Metropolis; Germany 1927; D: Fritz Lang; P: Erich Pommer; Sc: Thea von Harbou, Fritz Lang; DoP: Karl Freund, Günther Rittau; Cast: Alfred Abel, Gustav Fröhlich, Brigitte Helm, Rudolf Klein-Rogge, Fritz Rasp; B&W, 118 min. (DVD Edition).

Rank
60

SUNRISE: A SONG OF TWO HUMANS

Murnau's first US production combines Hollywood's state of the art with the artistic quality of German silent film. Movie tycoon William Fox had successfully lured the »German genius« to America by granting him absolute creative freedom, unlimited shooting time and an extremely generous budget. His new protégé used these resources to great effect, narrating a time- and placeless story about the nature of man. Staggering are the tableaus of city and country, lust and jealousy, hate and fear, loss and reconciliation, blissful happiness and the rebirth of a love that is as pure and radiant as a sunrise. To bring about this magnificent achievement, Murnau deploys everything he can get hold of: sensational tracking shots and montages, amazing crossfades and superimpositions, sceneries and constellations that recall the paintings of old masters, and incredibly sophisticated set and production designs. This may be silent cinema's peak moment, but it is also its swan song. 13 days after its US premiere, the first sound film THE JAZZ SINGER was released.

Sunrise: A Song of Two Humans; USA 1927; D: Friedrich Wilhelm Murnau; P: William Fox; Sc: Carl Mayer; DoP: Charles Rosher, Karl Struss; Cast: George O'Brien, Janet Gaynor, Margaret Livingston, Bodil Rosing, J. Farrell MacDonald; B&W, 95 min.

Rank
58

THE PASSION OF JOAN OF ARC

»Like a historical document from a time when cinema didn't exist,« said Jean Cocteau of Carl Theodor Dreyer's iconic and luminous interpretation of the passion of France's patron saint. It is indeed hard to believe that these fantastic, uncanny, strangely authentic images were made in the 20th century. As a source, Dreyer used the original records of the clerical tribunal against the young woman who was declared a heretic and burned at the stake in 1431. Although the film was shot in an elaborate movie set, Dreyer often choses close shots of the actors' faces in order to achieve a heightened emotionality suitable to its theme. The result is truly overwhelming. Dreyer contrasts the scorn and the cynical cruelty of the self-ag-

grandizing inquisitors with the vulnerability and humbleness of Joan of Arc, who will not even let go of her beliefs when the flames are reaching for her body. Maria Falconetti embodies this martyr in an awe-inspiring manner, full of fear and grief, pride and a sense of mission.

La passion de Jeanne d'Arc; France 1928; D: Carl Theodor Dreyer; Sc: Joseph Delteil, Carl Theodor Dreyer; DoP: Rudolph Maté; Cast: Maria Falconetti, Eugene Silvain, André Berley, Maurice Schutz, Antonin Artaud; B&W, 110 min. / 82 min. (DVD version).

Rank
86

CITY LIGHTS

In 1931, silent films had been pronounced dead and gone. People wanted talkies, wanted to see them and, above all, hear them. Nobody except Chaplin, who maintained his

skepticism about the new craze longer than anyone in Hollywood, would have dared to release a silent motion picture accompanied only by music and a handful of noise gags. But CITY LIGHTS became a major success and is regarded as one of Chaplin's best. As usual, the story is simple: the Little Tramp falls in love with a poor, blind flower girl. He tries to save her and her grandmother from being kicked out of their home and to find enough money to allow for eye surgery. Also, as usual, the film consists mainly of set pieces that would work just as well without a frame story. And yet, in this case, the whole is much more than the sum of its parts. The merit for this achievement belongs especially to the final scene in which the girl, now being able to see again, recognizes the Tramp as her selfless suitor. With their acting, Virginia Cherrill and Chaplin create a late monument in honor of silent cinema because, in this magical movie moment, words are completely unnecessary.

City Lights; USA 1931; D, P, Sc: Charles Chaplin; DoP: Gordon Pollock, Roland Totheroh; Cast: Charles Chaplin, Virginia Cherrill, Florence Lee, Harry Myers, Allan Garcia; B&W, 87 min.

Rank
44

M

Peter Lorre's child murderer, goggle-eyed and tormented by self-hatred, is the progenitor of Norman Bates, Hannibal Lecter et al.: the earliest psychopathic serial killer, an ambivalent villain both terrifying and pathetic. In Fritz Lang's first talkie, a film that instantly copes with the demands of sound and music in a masterful way, Lorre haunts Weimar Republic Berlin. Labeled »bogeyman«, he is giving the city's mothers sleepless nights, drives authorities to desperation and even causes the criminal community to start a collective search be-cause he obstructs their businesses. Lang manages to blend the crime plot with a most intensive background description while, thanks to a brilliant montage, at the same time revealing the parallels between bourgeois society and the world of organized crime. Although quite merciless in its depiction of the state of things, in the end, the film refuses to take sides. The bottom line is that we each have our reasons and that sometimes there are no winners.

M; Germany 1931; D: Fritz Lang; P: Seymour Nebenzal; Sc: Thea von Harbou, Fritz Lang; DoP: Fritz Arno Wagner; Cast: Peter Lorre, Gustav Gründgens, Otto Wernicke, Ernst Stahl-Nachbaur, Theo Lingen; B&W, 117 min. (premiere) / 110 min.

Rank
23

MODERN TIMES

This masterpiece is, at once, Chaplin's last silent film and his first sound film. Large parts of it are still silent or accompanied only with music, but, for the first time, spoken words are heard—announcements coming from loudspeakers as well as radio transmissions and phonograph recordings. Even the Tramp finds his voice for his last appearance on the big screen: he sings in a fantasy language, thus retaining the universal nature of his character. Grappling with the modern times of a mechanized working environment that reduces humans to machine-like entities serving at assem-

bly lines, Chaplin's beloved artistic figure once again pulls out all the stops. The ever-resilient little fellow inimitably fights with technology's pitfalls, unwillingly becomes a labor leader, artistically rides roller skates while being blindfolded and unabashedly skips out on a tab, ending up in jail again and again. But his last farewell is a triumph as he strides into a hopeful future with the adorable Paulette Goddard at his side. After that, it took Chaplin five years to re-invent himself for the modern times of cinema.

Modern Times; USA 1936; D, P, Sc: Charles Chaplin. DoP: Ira Morgan, Roland Totheroh; Cast: Charles Chaplin, Paulette Goddard, Henry Bergman, Stanley Sandford, Chester Conklin; B&W, 87 min.

Rank
66

GRAND ILLUSION

Jean Renoir's films move us because of their empathy for their characters. GRAND ILLUSION depicts the opponents of the First World War—Frenchmen, Germans, Englishmen, Russians—as men of

integrity, opposing the futile political chaos with dignity and honor. The film tells the story of a group of French prisoners of war who spend most of their time in different camps. The atmosphere is more reminiscent of a youth hostel, a world of practical jokes and pranks where even the guards are mild and sympathetic. Renoir's big talking point: borders do not

run between nations, but between social classes, with the upper class— on the German side, sublimely represented by the great Erich von Stroheim—painfully saying farewell to its aristocratic privileges. En passant, Renoir provides the prison movie genre with enough ideas and action patterns for a whole century.

La grande illusion; France 1937; D: Jean Renoir; P: Albert Pinkovitch, Frank Rollmer; Sc: Jean Renoir, Charles Spaak; DoP: Christian Matras; Cast: Jean Gabin, Dita Parlo, Pierre Fresnay, Erich von Stroheim, Marcel Dalio; B&W, 94 min. / 114 min. (reconstruction).

Rank
73

BRINGING UP BABY

For four years, uptight zoology professor David Huxley (Cary Grant) has been tinkering with his brontosaur skeleton and all that is missing to make him perfectly happy is one more bone. And, less importantly, marrying his cold and distant assistant. Has any comedy hero ever been more barking up the wrong tree? So, he gets what he deserves (and desperately needs): mishaps, accidents and breakdowns, a grotesque plush bathrobe in exchange for a torn tuxedo, and an escaped leopard which is by no means as tame as everybody believes. Life in all its color. And who does he owe it to? To eccentric and unconventional Susan Vance (Katharine Hepburn) who brings nothing but trouble, keeps her eyes glued to him and almost drives him to insanity. In a romantic comedy, teasing is a sign of affection, of course. Rarely has there been more affection. Howard Hawks celebrates this glorious nonsense with an unusual blend of high-speed pace and complete relaxation, bringing it all to a wonderful conclusion with a big bang.

Bringing Up Baby; USA 1938; D, P: Howard Hawks; Sc: Dudley Nichols, Hagar Wilde; DoP: Russell Metty; Cast: Katharine Hepburn, Cary Grant, Charles Ruggles, Walter Catlett, Barry Fitzgerald; B&W, 102 min.

Rank
89

THE RULES OF THE GAME

It doesn't come as a surprise that Robert Altman once re-marked that he had learned the rules of the game from THE RULES OF THE GAME. Jean Renoir's masterpiece is the ulti-mate ensemble film—a sensual round of love, a witty genre picture, a melancholic background description. World War II is never mentioned, but weighs heavily on the frivolous activities of a hunting party that is way too self-absorbed and busy with swapping partners to read the writing on the wall.

Renoir ele-gantly links a vast number of plot lines. His direction is precise and empathetic, and his visu-al concept is breathtaking. He captures the amusing goings-on with extremely long sequence shots, creates an enormous depth-of-field by playing with the relationship between foreground and background. His camera glides through the maze-like hunting lodge as if the steadycam had already been invented.

La règle du jeu; France 1939; D: Jean Renoir; Sc: Jean Renoir, Carl Koch; DoP: Jean-Paul Alphen, Jean Bachelet, Jacques Lemare, Alain Renoir; Cast: Nora Gregor, Paulette Dubost, Roland Toutain, Marcel Dalio, Jean Renoir; B&W, 110 min.

Rank
50

THE WIZARD OF OZ

Freud would have been delighted with this musical about the relation between dream and reality. Unlike Alice, a kindred spirit, over-anxious Dorothy doesn't fall down a rabbit's

hole, but is carried away by a tornado. Her destination is a Technicolor wonderland full of good and evil witches, mighty wizards and cute creatures like a talking Scarecrow, a heartless Tin Man and a cowardly Lion. Before she can find her way home, she has to overcome her fears, only to eventually realize that, like her three companions, all she needs she has carried within herself all along. The film deals with universal issues like home, family, growing up—and the weird logic of dreams. Most notably in the

United States, countless generations followed the *yellow brick road*, turning THE WIZARD OF OZ into an inherent, much-cited part of popular culture.

The Wizard of Oz; USA 1939; D: Victor Fleming; P: Mervin LeRoy; Sc: Noel Langley, Florence Ryerson, Edgar Allan Woolf; DoP: Harold Rosson; Cast: Judy Garland, Margaret Hamilton, Frank Morgan, Ray Bolger, Bert Lahr; B&W/Color, 101 min.

Rank
36

GONE WITH THE WIND

For decades, GONE WITH THE WIND was considered the highest-grossing film of all time. Successive generations were infatuated with David O'Selznick's adaptation of Margaret Mitchell's epic tale of the South that focuses on one of movie history's most colorful female characters. For almost four hours, farmer's daughter Scarlett O'Hara (Vivien Leigh), strong and

vain, heroic and immature, fights for love and survival. She drools over Ashley (Leslie Howard), a man beyond reach, marries the wrong guy twice and the right one in the end: charming philanderer Rhett Butler (Clark Gable) with whom she skirmishes enjoyably. It's not a minute too long. One gets enthusiastic about the movie's enormous production value and irresistible pace. Elegantly, it blends personal and historical drama when depicting—regardless of any kind of political correctness—the unrest of the American Civil War. Along the way, a selfish life plan is destroyed and the headstrong heroine is finally forced to come to maturity.

Gone with the Wind; USA 1939; D: Victor Fleming; P: David O. Selznick; Sc: Sidney Howard; DoP: Ernest Haller; Cast: Vivien Leigh, Clark Gable, Leslie Howard, Olivia de Havilland, Thomas Mitchell; Color, 224 min.

Rank
28

CITIZEN KANE

CITIZEN KANE is more like a cubistic portrait than your average biopic. It's like a jigsaw puzzle that can never be solved entirely. And an essay about the possibilities and limitations of cinematic narration. In a most intricate way, it tells us about the life of newspaper tycoon Charles Foster Kane, a charismatic and enigmatic character portrayed by rookie director Orson Welles, then only 26 years old, but already a radio and theater legend. He wasn't the first filmmaker to use

flashbacks, sequence shots or deep focus, but still, the film gives the impression that he invented these devices all the same. Welles handles time and space in a most elegant manner, he unleashes the camera and paints with shadows and light. But for all its stylistic bravura, CITIZEN KANE is not about moviemaking technique at all. It's about emotions and deep human insights: a monument of cinema history.

Citizen Kane; USA 1941; D, P: Orson Welles; Sc: Herman J. Mankiewicz, Orson Welles; DoP: Gregg Toland; Cast: Orson Welles, Joseph Cotten, Dorothy Comingore, Agnes Moorehead, Everett Sloane; B&W, 119 min.

Rank
1

THE MALTESE FALCON

It took Warner Bros. three attempts before the studio finally succeeded in distilling Dashiell Hammett's great detective novel into a worthy screen adaptation. John Huston and Humphrey Bogart deliver the real Sam Spade, defining the private eye in an exciting new way: cold and distanced, unpredictable and resourceful, hard-boiled, yet still full of self-doubt, not a saint, but a man with principles. Bogart is magnificent against equally strong performances by his opponents. Mary Astor as an inscrutable beauty, Peter Lorre as a bohemian oddball and Sydney Greenstreet as a dangerous fat man are greedy, egocentric characters hunting after the eponymous bird sculpture as if it was the Holy Grail.

The movie achieves a pace that far exceeds most of today's productions. Not a second is wasted, the editing flawless, each line of dialog drives the plot forward. Huston's furious debut, regarded as the first true film noir, is a wonderful example of the level of quality the studio system was able to achieve if it really made an effort.

The Maltese Falcon; USA 1941; D, Sc: John Huston; P: Hal B. Wallis; DoP: Arthur Edeson; Cast: Humphrey Bogart, Mary Astor, Peter Lorre, Sydney Greenstreet, Barton MacLane; B&W, 101 min.

Rank
91

CASABLANCA

You must remember this. Play it again, Sam. Kiss me as if it were the last time. Here's looking at you, kid. I think this is the beginning of a beautiful friendship.—CASABLANCA,

movie history's ultimate melodrama, is overflowing with familiar quotations, mythical moments, legendary places. The love triangle in the center is pure magic. There's Humphrey Bogart, a cynic still suffering after having lost the love of his life. There's Ingrid Bergman, gorgeous but at odds with herself. And there's Paul Henreid, an upright member of the Résistance. During the turmoil of World War II, their personal affairs intertwine with the courses of the world, and the result is a riot of emotion, most elegantly staged by director Michael Curtiz. The final scene is a screen legend and another unforgettable moment. By setting Bergman's Ilsa free on the fog-shrouded airport, Bogart's Rick finally redeems himself. *A sigh is just a sigh.*

Casablanca; USA 1943; D: Michael Curtiz; P: Hal B. Wallis; Sc: Julius J. Epstein, Philip G. Epstein, Howard Koch; DoP: Arthur Edeson; Cast: Humphrey Bogart, Ingrid Bergman, Paul Henreid, Claude Rains, Conrad Veidt; B&W, 102 min.

Rank
9

DOUBLE INDEMNITY

What a wicked game this is, a cynical tale about greed and seduction, fraud and murder. For years, the insurance salesman Walter Neff (Fred MacMurray) has toyed with his idea for the perfect crime. When he meets Phyllis Dietrichson (Barbara Stanwyck), a femme fatale if there ever was one, his pipe dream unexpectedly turns into a plan as he succumbs to her charms and agrees to kill her husband. If they can make it look like an accident, Walter's company will double the payout thanks to a special clause in the contract. But soon after the deed is done, Walter cannot hear his own steps anymore and feels »like a dead man«. He is not mistaken, his fate is sealed. An absence of light characterizes the world of film noir, a style that Billy Wilder helped to define with this immaculate thriller. Darkness acts as an accomplice of the figures, encouraging their criminal behavior

while imprisoning them in a menacing web of shadows. Further typical Noir elements such as flashbacks and voice-over narration add to the gloomy feeling of fatalism that echoes the disenchanted attitude of its time.

Double Indemnity; USA 1944; D: Billy Wilder; P: Buddy G. DeSylva (uncredited); Sc: Billy Wilder, Raymond Chandler; DoP: John F. Seitz; Cast: Fred MacMurray, Barbara Stanwyck, Edward G. Robinson, Porter Hall, Jean Heather; B&W, 107 min.

Rank
72

CHILDREN OF PARADISE

According to François Truffaut, Marcel Carné's major directing achievement is no auteur movie but an »equipe movie«: the awe-inspiring result of a collaboration under adverse conditions. Shot during the final years of the Sec-

ond World War when official French film production had come to a halt, CHILDREN OF PARADISE is a tremendous effort which brings the Parisian theater world of the 19th century to life. It is a landmark of Poetic Realism centring on a beautiful actress (Arletty) who is idolized by many men, but incapable of real love. The film takes its time to establish characters and social background; parts of the story are based on true events. What

makes it so special is not only the beauty of the images or the grandeur of the actors' performances, but the sophisticated interplay between stage and reality. Moving!

Les enfants du paradis; France 1943-45; D: Marcel Carné; P: André Paulve; Sc: Jacques Prévert; DoP: Roger Hubert, Marc Fossard; Cast: Arletty, Jean-Louis Barrault, Pierre Brasseur, Marcel Herrand, Louis Salou; B&W, 189 min.

Rank
85

IT'S A WONDERFUL LIFE

No matter how many times you have seen it, it seems impossible not to fall in love again with the charm, the warmth and the humanity of Frank Capra's classic Christmas picture. Sometimes, all that sentiment may be applied a little too lavishly, but the emotional power, especially of James Stewart's performance, is beyond reproach. For a long time, the story of kind-hearted George Bailey lingers in a pleasant comfort zone of small-town idyll.  But just when serenity finds its way into the life of the hero, who always yearned for adventures in far-away places but stayed home in cozy Bedford Falls out of altruism, fate pulls the rug out from under his feet in the final act. How Stewart plays the bottomless despair in which the alleged unshakable optimist plunges is unforgettable. Heavenly intervention is needed to get him out of there and to make him realize that there is a meaning to his life after all. After the grave times of the Great Depression and the Second World War, this universal message was a much-needed remedy for the minds not only of Americans; it remains so until today. A hymn to life, in good times and bad.

It's a Wonderful Life; USA 1946; D, P: Frank Capra; Sc: Frances Goodrich, Albert Hackett, Frank Capra; DoP: Joseph F. Biroc, Joseph Walker; Cast: James Stewart, Donna Reed, Thomas Mitchell, Henry Travers, Lionel Barrymore; B&W, 130 min.

Rank
34

BICYCLE THIEVES

It's hard to believe but, by a fraction of an inch, BICYCLE THIEVES would have been a Hollywood movie, produced by David O'Selznick and starring Cary Grant. In the end, director Vittorio De Sica changed his mind because he wanted to pursue a different concept. He wanted his postwar Rome, a

place defined by poverty and unemployment, as authentic as possible and abandoned all professional actors and studio sets. The result is one of the most significant works of Italian Neorealism, a powerful drama that is, at the same time, a gripping document of a desperate era and a moving parable. De Sica turns the hopeless search for a bicycle into the odyssey of a father who, together with his infant son, gets caught up in the maelstrom of big city life and is confronted with a vast variety of human emotions. It is a sheer fight for survival in a society in which dignity and integrity are as relative as guilt and wrongdoing.

Ladri di biciclette; Italy 1948; D: Vittorio De Sica; P: Giuseppe Amato; Sc: Cesare Zavattini; DoP: Carlo Montuori; Cast: Lamberto Maggiorani, Enzo Staiola, Lianella Carell, Gino Saltamerenda, Vittorio Antonucci; B&W, 93 min.

Rank
54

THE THIRD MAN

It's all about atmosphere in this British Noir classic which is still part of the standard repertoire of London's arthouse cinemas. In order to get the peculiar feel of bombed-out, sectorized post-war Vienna exactly right, author Graham Greene especially wrote a novel that served him as a reference for his script. Carol Reed shot a large part of the scenes on location; among the cast are the famous Austrian character actors Paul Hörbiger and Erich Ponto, and Viennese German is spoken frequently. All of this pays off. Not many pictures compare to this one when it comes to coherence, density and authentic flair. But it holds

even more aces: tilted camera angles, perfectly composed images, ambitious montages and the unforgettable zither score of Anton Karas all help to conjure up a constant, alluring air of menace and foreboding. Joseph Cotten impresses as a laconic novelist who suspects that the death of his friend was no accident. Alida Valli gives an inspired performance as a sophisticated and broken-hearted beauty. And Orson Welles turns his few minutes of screen time as an unprincipled black-market profiteer into an event. Harry Lime may be dead, but THE THIRD MAN lives on.

The Third Man; UK 1949; D, P: Carol Reed; Sc: Graham Greene; DoP: Robert Krasker; Cast: Joseph Cotten, Alida Valli, Orson Welles, Trevor Howard, Bernard Lee; B&W, 104 min.

Rank
21

SUNSET BLVD.

The dream factory as a nightmare: Billy Wilder and his partner Charles Brackett take a remarkably honest look behind the glamorous façades of Tinseltown in this drama about a failed screenwriter and a long forgotten diva of the

silent era. The film begins with William Holden as a corpse floating face-down in a swimming pool, commencing to tell the story of his fatal encounter with the once celebrated star, Norma Desmond. Wilder's casting choice for this solitary figure, who has been living in seclusion in her decaying mansion for ages, but still dreams of a return to the spotlight, is a stroke of genius. Gloria Swanson used to be one of the biggest screen icons of the 1920s herself. She plays Desmond's life as if it was her own. The inclusion of other Hollywood survivors, such as Cecil B. DeMille, Buster Keaton and Hedda Hopper, but especially of Erich von Stroheim who plays Desmond's ex-husband, now downgraded to a butler, provides the tragic story with additional weight and authenticity. Endowed with a lot of inside knowledge and shot in exquisite black and white, it is an apt farewell to a time that even in the 1950s seemed to be a mythical and distant era.

Sunset Blvd.; USA 1950; D: Billy Wilder; P: Charles Brackett; Sc: Charles Brackett, Billy Wilder, D.M. Marshman Jr.; DoP: John F. Seitz; D: William Holden, Gloria Swanson, Erich von Stroheim, Nancy Olson, Fred Clark; B&W, 110 min.

Rank
29

RASHOMON

It's horrible that there is no such thing as »the truth«, says one of the three men who seek shelter from the rain underneath the city gate, mulling over the meaning of a certain story. It is a tale of rape and murder; but nobody knows what really happened in the ominous bosquet. The film uses the rhetorical device of indirect speech: the lumberjack and the monk each report on a trial during which every witness claims to have seen a different killer. Thus, RASHOMON develops into a fascinating discourse about truth and lies, deception and self-deceit. Kurosawa directs each episode in a different style. By confronting any alleged objectivity with new facts and chang-

ing perspectives, he enriches the cinematic vocabulary: it is a narrative style which deals with the power and the limitations of narration in itself. The fourth version also doesn't deliver any reliable information, but, as the servant has it, you can lie as much as you want as long as your story is well told.

Rashômon; Japan 1950; D: Akira Kurosawa; P: Minoru Jingo; Sc: Akira Kurosawa, Shinobu Hashimoto; DoP: Kazuo Miyagawa; Cast: Toshirô Mifune, Machiko Kyô, Masayuki Takashi Shimura, Minoru Chiaki, Kichijiro Ueda; B&W, 88 min.

Rank
45

ALL ABOUT EVE

SUNSET BLVD. and ALL ABOUT EVE are two sides of the same coin. In 1950, they both hit American cinemas within months, each telling the story of a screen legend's involuntary decline. In Billy Wilder's film noir, Gloria Swanson

plays the aging diva; in Joseph L. Mankiewicz's portrait of the theater world, the great Bette Davis confronts her eccentric termagant with a more realistic version. Susceptible to flattery of all kinds, the Broadway star hires Anne Baxter, one of her biggest fans, as an understudy. But the alleged wallflower has, in fact, no other goal than to take her heroine's place. Mankiewicz's direction, depicting the machinery of a mean wire-pulling, is full of smart and sarcastic dialogue. At the same time, the film paints a sophisticated picture of New York's Broadway scene with all its malice and vanities. The beguilingly young Marilyn Monroe, on the brink of a becoming a runaway success in Hollywood, sticks out of a phenomenal ensemble for a handful of scenes.

All About Eve; USA 1950; D, Sc: Joseph L. Mankiewicz; P: Daryl F. Zanuck; DoP: Milton Krasner; Cast: Bette Davis, Anne Baxter, George Sanders, Thelma Ritter, Marilyn Monroe; B&W, 138 min.

Rank
43

SINGIN' IN THE RAIN

Even musical-haters are known to be admirers of this genre milestone. Its origins didn't seem all that promising. Arthur Freed, owner of the rights to a dozen random songs he and Nacio Herb Brown had written over the years, came up with the idea to put them all together for a musical. The authors handled this challenge with bravura and wrote a scintillating script that perfectly showcases the stars of the movie, especially Gene Kelly, who passes his triple assignment as leading man, co-director and choreographer with flying colors.

The story revolves around a vain silent movie hero struggling to make the transition to talking films. Its wit and clever structure elevate it to being much more than a mere framework for the staging of the songs. The performers are outdoing themselves, the songs are irresistible and have long since become classics, the dance numbers and choreographies are a feast for the eyes—this is genuine great art, moving on nimble feet.

Singin' in the Rain; USA 1952; D: Gene Kelly, Stanley Donen; P: Arthur Freed; Sc: Adolph Green, Betty Comden; DoP: Harold Rosson; D: Gene Kelly, Donald O'Connor, Debbie Reynolds, Jean Hagen, Millard Mitchell; Color, 103 min.

Rank
10

TOKYO STORY

A Japanese version of cinema that seems to come not only from different shores, but from a another world, apparently artless and unadorned, and yet stylistically accomplished and possessing absolute formal rigor. Yasujirô Ozu was convinced that the mundane lives of ordinary people hold all the depth and drama a film needs to captivate an audience. TOKYO STORY confirms this notion admirably. Its modest family story unfolds little by little into a nuanced and touching depiction of life's joys and sorrows, of its banalities and complexities. The camera always assumes the

same position of a person sitting, registering everything that takes place in contemplative tranquility. When he shows a conversation, Ozu cuts the speakers against each other in unusual 180-degree angles of frontal opposition. These scenes are punctuated by city perspectives and landscape shots. For the unpracticed viewer, this can take some getting used to, but it very effectively encourages the concentration on what is essential. A fascinating counterdraft to Hollywood's often bold and simple eye-catching aesthetics.

Tôkyô monogatari; Japan 1953; D: Yasujirô Ozu; P: Takeshi Yamamoto; Sc: Kôgo Noda, Yasujirô Ozu; DoP: Yûharu Atsuta; Cast: Chishû Ryû, Chieko Higashiyama, Setsuko Hara, Haruko Sugimura, Sô Yamamura; B&W, 136 min.

Rank
31

SEVEN SAMURAI

Though bold, noble and opulent, this heroic epic still comes across as a work of unpretentious modesty. The plot, clean-cut and straight, supplies a familiar pattern for countless westerns, ac-tion movies and adventure tales: after being repeatedly mugged by bandits, rice farmers in 17th century Japan hire a group of samurai to protect their village, prepare them for the next battle against the villains and, finally, destroy the enemy, involving heavy losses. It's a tale of dignity. Akira Kurosawa portrays the historic fighters and their proud, but lonely existence on the margins of society. Each and every detail of his direction is superb: the thrilling force of combat, nature's lyrical beauty, the clever characterizations, the sublime use of fast and slow motion. And in the thick of it: Toshiro Mifune, a dancing whirlwind.

Shichinin no samurai; Japan 1954; D: Akira Kurosawa; P: Sojiro Motoki; Sc: Akira Kurosawa, Shinobu Hashimoto, Hideo Oguni; DoP: Asakazu Nakai; Cast: Takashi Shimura, Toshirô Mifune, Yoshio Inaba, Seiji Miyaguchi, Minoru, Chiaki; B&W, 206 min.

Rank
16

ON THE WATERFRONT

A landmark of socio-critical cinema. On the one hand, the story of dock worker Terry Malloy (Marlon Brando), who reluctantly unchains himself from the clutches of a corrupt union, works as a parable about moral and justice. On the

other hand, it is the document of an era in which political conflict was argued out with one's fists. With his gripping drama, Elia Kazan, probably Hollywood's most controversial left-wing director, succeeds not only as a dedicated maker of political movies, but also as a great actors' director who knows how to charm a great cast into delivering even greater accomplishments. That applies for roguish Lee J. Cobb in the role of a Mafia don, for gentle Karl Malden as a fearless priest, and for angelic Eva Marie Saint as an upright young woman investigating a murder so thoroughly that the whole power structure of Hoboken's port operations finally collapses. And it specifically applies for Brando, whose »I coulda been a contenda« soliloquy belongs to movie history's mythical moments. With ON THE WATERFRONT, he established himself once and for all as an exceptional artist with an extremely intense method.

On the Waterfront; USA 1954; D: Elia Kazan; P: Sam Spiegel; Sc: Budd Schulberg; DoP: Boris Kaufman; Cast: Marlon Brando, Lee J. Cobb, Eva Marie Saint, Karl Malden, Rod Steiger; B&W, 108 min.

Rank
61

REAR WINDOW

An apartment, a courtyard, a man in a wheelchair and a murder—Hitchcock fuses these ingredients into a profound reflection on the voyeur in us all and man's insatiable need for knowledge. In the windows across a backyard in New York's Greenwich Village, the master of suspense presents us with a panopticon of human relationships, narrating large parts of the story exclusively in images. Using point-of-view shots, he shows us what the hero (James Stewart) sees, thus persuading us to believe him, unlike the police, that a crime has actually taken place. Not taken seriously by his cop friend, he continues his investigations handicapped and alone, although present-ly joined by his fiancée (a rav-ishingly beauti-ful Grace Kelly).

Behind the telephoto lens of his camera, the photo reporter turns into a peeping tom, torn between curiosity and feel-ings of guilt. Unable to justify his behavior, even to the murderer, he still has to carry on. With cinema's very own means, this film elucidates like few others that we believe what we see.

Rear Window; USA 1954; D, P: Alfred Hitchcock; Sc: John Michael Hayes; DoP: Robert Burks; Cast: James Stewart, Grace Kelly, Wendell Corey, Thelma Ritter, Raymond Burr; Color, 112 min.

THE NIGHT OF THE HUNTER

In a way, Charles Laughton's sole directorial contribution to cinema is pure visual poetry, spiritually akin to the magical realism of García Márquez's writing, and yet it tells a very straightforward story of greed, murder, and benevolence. Robert Mitchum's portrayal of a terrifying psychopathic priest, who has the words »Love« and »Hate« tattooed on the knuckles of his hands, might be his strongest performance ever. To get hold of a loot of 10,000 dollars hidden inside a doll, he hunts after two little children, the heroes of this movie. Fleeing from the lethal grip of this madman,

the defenseless orphans travel across an economically languishing country, discovering a world of wonders through innocent eyes along the way. In line with the story's magical tone, they stick together in steadfast sibling love until nature and civilization form a mystical alliance that eventually carries them into safety. Inspired by the German expressionism of the silent era, Laughton devises images of unforgettable intensity and sublime beauty that have to be seen to be believed.

The Night of the Hunter; USA 1955; D: Charles Laughton; P: Paul Gregory; Sc: James Agee; DoP: Stanley Cortez; Cast: Robert Mitchum, Shelley Winters, Lillian Gish, Billy Chapin, Sally Jane Bruce; B&W, 93 min.

Rank
62

THE SEARCHERS

In this John Ford western, John Wayne is as fierce as a dragon, a grim misanthrope whose Homeric odyssey is driven by hatred and hunger for revenge. It is all a matter of losing—and defending—one's home, of the contrast between civilization and wilderness, of the westerner relentlessly doing what has to be done. Monument Valley with its bizarre buttes is one of the main characters here, a majestic  landscape with a nostalgic glow. But it is during the scenes set in the settlers' houses that director John Ford truly celebrates the American foundation myth and the vigor of the young nation. However, beneath its patriotic surface, THE SEARCHERS has a lot to say about racism, chauvinism and personality. It's a sophisticated story—with one exception. As in so many westerns of the time, the Native Americans are depicted as ruthless villains. Ford later apologized to them for ignoring the historical facts and using them as primitive bad guys.

The Searchers; USA 1956; D: John Ford; P: C.V. Whitney; Sc: Frank S. Nugent; DoP: Winton C. Hoch; Cast: John Wayne, Jeffrey Hunter, Henry Brandon, Vera Miles, Natalie Wood; Color, 119 min.

Rank
27

1957

THE SEVENTH SEAL

An allegory about human existence in the guise of a medieval mystery play. When the knight Antonius Block returns from a crusade to his Swedish homeland after ten years, life

feels like purgatory to him. After all the atrocities he witnessed, he can neither live nor die without being certain of God's existence. When Death comes to take him, he wrests a postponement from the Grim Reaper for the duration of a chess match, hoping to perform »one meaningful deed« before it is too late. While the game continues, Block and his sardonic squire Jöns move across the plague-ridden country. On their way, they encounter frightened inhabitants, make friends with travelling artists, witness a flagellation ritual and the burning of an alleged witch. Block still hopes for an epiphany, while Jöns considers his master's soul-searching monologues to be worthless drivel. Bergman and his ensemble transform the screen into a theater stage, Gunnar Fischer's photography paints pictures of archaic force. Death may be the final instance, but, as Bergman shows us at the end, life comes first.

Det sjunde inseglet; Sweden 1957; D, Sc: Ingmar Bergman; P: Allan Ekelund; DoP: Gunnar Fischer; Cast: Max von Sydow, Gunnar Björnstrand, Bengt Ekerot, Bibi Andersson, Nils Poppe; B&W, 96 min.

Rank
76

TOUCH OF EVIL

The first shot is a screen legend. It starts with a bomb in close-up and ends, a good three minutes later, with its detonation. In between lies one of the most complex tracking shots of the pre-computer era, a virtuoso floating and sliding through the sinful bordertown of Los Robles. With this beginning, Orson Welles leads us right into the heart of a nightmarish conflict personified by two very opposing police detectives. On the one side, there is an upright Mexican (Charlton Heston), on the other, a corrupt and dirty American (Welles as a walrus-like sleazeball). Their fight is set in a confusing story maze full of

dark alleys from which there is no escape. Not for the good guy who has the law and the moral on his side, but still can't prevail. Nor for the bad guy who holds the upper hand even after his death. Here, classic film noir that had been established as a Hollywood style 17 years before by THE MALTESE FALCON, comes to its diabolic conclusion.

Touch of Evil; USA 1958; D, Sc: Orson Welles; P: Albert Zugsmith; DoP: Russell Metty; Cast: Charlton Heston, Janet Leigh, Orson Welles, Marlene Dietrich, Akim Tamiroff; B&W, 95/111 min.

Rank
57

VERTIGO

The opening titles by Saul Bass anticipate the spiral shape of things to come. Hitchcock's plot is unparalleled, an outrageous series of surprise twists where nothing is as it seems. James Stewart's Scottie, an ex-cop suffering from extreme fear of heights, is an obsessive hero and by no means your average pleasant guy. He falls for a mysterious blonde (Kim Novak), witnesses her death, then desperately tries to mold another woman into her. The truth of the matter is that he is not acting but being acted. Step by step, he helps to put a sinister plan into practice. He's heading for disaster, urgently, and when he finally sees the light, it's too late to avert

it. VERTIGO makes your head spin, it's a tricky, multilayered film that alternately works like a thriller, a romantic drama and a feverish dream. The long tracking shots are hypnotic, they pull us right into the dramatic maze. Bernard Herrmann's score is beautiful and menacing. And Hitchcock's directing stunts are revolutionary. During the heyday of Hollywood's studio system, films couldn't get more personal than this. Calling it PSYCHO would have been appropriate even then.

Vertigo; USA 1958; D, P: Alfred Hitchcock; Sc: Alec Coppel, Samuel Taylor; DoP: Robert Burks; Cast: James Stewart, Kim Novak, Barbara Bel Geddes, Tom Helmore, Henry Jones; Color, 128 min.

SOME LIKE IT HOT

Two penniless musicians in prohibition-era Chicago involuntarily become witnesses of a Mob murder. In a spur-of-the-moment decision, they slip into women's clothes, join a girl's jazz band and take off to Florida where things get really out of hand. What sounds like a blend of machine-gun blasts and bawdy sex jokes, gangster farce and frivolous comedy is precisely that. And yet, it is so much more—but why, exactly? Is it Billy Wilder's confident direction that allows not one weak spot during these flawless two hours? Is it the immaculate script or the brilliant black-and-white  photography? The infectious performances by Tony Curtis, Jack Lemmon and their fellow actors? Or is it Marilyn Monroe's inexplicable, irresistible and radiant screen presence after all? All we know for sure is that all its elements team up to raise this picture far above most comedies Hollywood has spawned since, including Wilder's own oeuvre. The famous last line of this immortal classic claims that »Nobody's perfect.« Well, cinema sometimes is.

Some Like It Hot; USA 1959; D, P: Billy Wilder; Sc: Billy Wilder, I.A.L. Diamond; DoP: Charles Lang Jr.; Cast: Marilyn Monroe, Tony Curtis, Jack Lemmon, George Raft, Pat O'Brien; B&W, 120 min.

Rank
8

THE 400 BLOWS

Between childhood and adulthood lies the no man's land of puberty. Life in this often bleak zone is described by François Truffaut in his acclaimed first film, using the example

of a twelve-year-old from Paris. Antoine Doinel experiences no love from his mother and his stepfather. He lives barely above the poverty line and is maltreated by authoritarian teachers. Sometimes, he breaks out of this tristesse, skipping school, secretly smoking cigarettes and watching adventure movies at the theater. When a theft is added to his tall tales, his help- and heartless mother puts him into a correction facility. But Antoine escapes again—to the sea, and into an uncertain future, which unfolds in several Doinel sequels by Truffaut. Without clichés and sentimentality, THE 400 BLOWS delineates the nuisances of adolescence, a time adults like to idealize as »the best in life.« Leading actor Jean-Pierre Léaud became the alter ego of a filmmaker who never championed the heroes, but whose heart went out to the losers, the misfits, the outsiders.

Les quatre cents coups; France 1959; D, P, Sc: François Truffaut; DoP: Henri Decaë; Cast: Jean-Pierre Léaud, Claire Maurier, Albert Rémy, Patrick Auffay, Guy Decomble; B&W, 99 min.

Rank
46

NORTH BY NORTHWEST

It was Ernest Lehman's stated aim to write the quintessential Hitchcock picture. In the course of dozens of conversations, Hitch himself made sure that Lehman's wish gradually became a reality. From the title sequence, congenially created by Saul Bass, to the very last shot known as film history's most famous coitus metaphor, this thriller contains everything associated with perfect movie entertainment—a mesmerizing story, a swift pace, breathtaking settings, subtle sex, sublime humor, splendid actors and a mise-en-scène that brings all these ingredients to full fruition. The ten-minute cornfield sequence fea-

turing Cary Grant running for dear life while being attacked from a crop duster remains a lesson in timing and suspense. Hitchcock's favorite characters—the average man who gets into life-threatening trouble because of a mistaken identity and the mysterious, coolly erotic blonde who promises temptation, but also mischief—have never been combined to greater effect. That they are complemented by a complex, even sympathetic villain is the icing on the cake.

USA 1959; D: Alfred Hitchcock; P: Alfred Hitchcock, Herbert Coleman; Sc: Ernest Lehman; DoP: Robert Burks; Cast: Cary Grant, Eva Marie Saint, James Mason, Martin Landau, Leo G. Carroll; Color, 136 min.

LA DOLCE VITA

In 1960, Federico Fellini decided to leave neo-realism behind for good and try something entirely new. What he came up with was so unexpected, so bold and magnificent

that it is no exaggeration to say that the world had never seen anything like it before. LA DOLCE VITA is an episodic selection of sequences and striking images fueled by inexhaustible creativity, at the same time, hedonistic and socio-critical and shot in addictive black and white. Marcello Mastroianni slips into the role of Fellini's alter ego for the first time here. He plays a celebrity reporter in an economically thriving post-war Rome who halfheartedly looks for a deeper meaning in life, but is all too easily distracted by shiny surfaces and glamorous appearances such as the Swedish bombshell Anita Ekberg. He represents an attitude predominant in a city full of exciting attractions and seemingly endless possibilities, suppressing the uncomfortable business of having to deal with existential questions. Incapable of love, he remains eternally disappointed, chasing for the sweet life, but never able to shake off its bitter aftertaste.

La dolce vita; Italy/France 1960; D: Federico Fellini; P: Giuseppe Amato, Franco Magli; Sc: Federico Fellini, Ennio Flaiano, Tullio Pinelli, Brunello Rondi; DoP: Otello Martelli; Cast: Marcello Mastroianni, Anita Ekberg, Anouk Aimée, Yvonne Furneaux, Magali Noël; B&W, 174 min.

Rank
65

BREATHLESS

A small story with a big impact. Jean-Luc Godard broke with all the rules of traditional filmmaking in his debut, pushing the door for a new kind of cinema wide open. Jump cuts, hand-held camera shots and an authentic street language lend this gangster ballad with an existential touch a feeling of immediacy, nonchalance and playfulness that is still fresh today. In spite of its iconoclasm, Hollywood is quoted or referenced in almost every single shot. Delightful in his cockiness, Jean-Paul Belmondo plays the ever-smoking Bogart admirer and small-time crook Michel, who becomes a cop killer

in the same casual way in which he later discards his own life. Jean Seberg's Patricia became a role model for the autonomous, sexually liberated young woman of the 1960s. Shot on location all over Paris, the story takes place on the Champs-Élysées, in public buildings and tiny hotel rooms. This was made possible by DoP Raoul Coutard's ability to carry the heavy 35 mm camera on his shoulder even for long stretches. Just like Belmondo's body, the images are always in motion, unleashed and free from all constraints.

À bout de souffle; France 1960; D, Sc: Jean-Luc Godard; P: Georges de Beauregard; DoP: Raoul Coutard; Cast: Jean-Paul Belmondo, Jean Seberg, Daniel Boulanger, Jean-Pierre Melville, Henri-Jacques Huet; B&W, 87 min.

Rank
51

L'AVVENTURA

1960: in France, Godard storms the silver screen; in the US, Hitchcock revolutionizes the thriller; in Italy, Fellini ventures into uncharted territory, and his compatriot Michelangelo Antonioni radically breaks with filmic conventions.

What if a movie would offer no final answers, just like real life? No psychologizing, no narrative closure, only openness, ambivalence and possibility? Truth expresses itself in the relation between the actors and their surroundings, the landscape and architecture, their distance to each other, their looks and movements. Similar to PSYCHO, the female protagonist disappears half an hour into the movie, but, contrary to Hitchcock, Antonioni withholds the explanation. Like actors in a Beckett play, the missing girl's friends scramble over the tiny, barren and windswept island, to find nothing. Was it a spontaneous whim that made her vanish, a sudden mood swing after a quarrel with her fiancé, an accident? Without a conclusion, the unsettling event quickly loses its gravity. Everybody returns to their agendas, ready to forget, to face forward and to take advantage of the situation. The past is gone, the future uncertain: an adventure.

L'avventura; Italy/France 1960; D: Michelangelo Antonioni; P: Amato Pennasilico; Sc: Michelangelo Antonioni, Elio Bartolini, Tonino Guerra; DoP: Aldo Scavarda; Cast: Gabriele Ferzetti, Monica Vitti, Lea Massari, Dominique Blanchar, Renzo Ricci; B&W, 143 min.

Rank
96

THE APARTMENT

Depending on your point of view, THE APARTMENT is either the most depressing comedy or the funniest tragedy of all time. Billy Wilder's final Oscar triumph (five Awards, ten nominations) wondrously balances out drama and grotesque, satire and romance. New York's business world is depicted as a mass assembly of poor characters: the privileged are taking advantage of their power while the rest prostitute themselves unscrupulously just to get ahead. Jack Lemmon's feisty and spineless »Buddy Boy« only manages to climb the corporate ladder because he provides a love nest for his superiors. His daily routine is a complete mess, but

things get worse when his colleague Shirley MacLaine, who's the mistress of big boss Fred MacMurray, tries to commit suicide in the eponymous apartment. There's not much room to delude oneself considering the moral premise: in this frosty world, there's no good or evil, no black or white—at best, a little comfort for the grey in the middle.

The Apartment; USA 1960; D, P: Billy Wilder; Sc: Billy Wilder, I.A.L. Diamond; DoP: Joseph LaShelle; Cast: Jack Lemmon, Shirley MacLaine, Fred MacMurray, Ray Walston, Jack Kruschen; B&W, 120 min.

Rank
38

PSYCHO

No other thriller has deceived and manipulated us as perfectly as PSYCHO. During act one, it seems as if Marion Crane (Janet Leigh) is our main protagonist. She's hardly

what would have been labeled a decent girl at the time. She has sex on her lunch break, steals a few thousand dollars from her boss, then pops off into what could be a new life. But what a surprise when she is slaughtered by shy motel-owner Norman Bates' mother under the shower right in the middle of the story! Having barely assimilated that information, we already start siding with Norman (Anthony Perkins). Doesn't he look so confused when cleaning up the bloodbath, allegedly to protect his mother? We even share the thrill with him when Marion's car refuses to bog down in the swamp behind the motel. But no, we don't want detective Arbogast (Martin Balsam) to be killed who soon becomes the second stabbing victim. When Lila Crane (Vera Miles), finally, swings around that chair, uncovering mother's rotten skull, it's the most shocking moment of them all: the mother of all plot twists, so to speak. PSYCHO is the ultimate Hitchcock roller coaster ride—and striking proof that you can do big things on a small budget.

Psycho; USA 1960; D, P: Alfred Hitchcock; Sc: Joseph Stephano; DoP: John L. Russell; Cast: Anthony Perkins, Janet Leigh, Vera Miles, John Gavin, Martin Balsam; B&W, 109 min.

Rank
13

LAWRENCE OF ARABIA

For T.E. Lawrence, nothing is written. It is not only allowed, it is an obligation even to rebel against narrow-minded superiors, superstitious tribal chiefs, the desert with all its pitfalls and obstacles. Thus, the British officer achieves the impossible during World War I: he unites the Arab world, wins hopeless battles, and becomes a legend. For Peter O'Toole, this shrouded in myth character is the role of a lifetime. He's all boyish charm, a charismatic, obsessive dandy who rel-

ishes his uniqueness, while at the same time suffering from it. Lasting almost four hours and shining with extravagance and luxurious production values, David Lean's epos is still a character study at heart: a bold portrait of an unusual man. Lean doesn't care much about the rules of the war movie genre (or the advantages of female speaking parts, for that matter). Though a complex and complicated film, LAWRENCE OF ARABIA still blooms in lyrical, almost spiritual beauty. It's a sensual experience without equal in cinema history.

Lawrence of Arabia; UK 1962; D: David Lean; P: Sam Spiegel; Sc: Robert Bolt, Michael Wilson; DoP: F.A. Young; Cast: Peter O'Toole, Omar Sharif, Anthony Quinn, Alec Guinness, Jack Hawkins; Color, 216 min. / 228 min. (restoration).

Rank
14

8 1/2

Although his last film was a triumph, a middle-aged director (Marcello Mastroianni) becomes lost. Somehow, something is missing: he has no artistic vision, no emotional

determination. While in the seclusion of a sanatorium, he falls between the cracks: between art and commerce, ambition and indifference, marriage and affair, past and present. Fellini, himself directing his »eight and halfth« movie, creates an intricate revue in which his brooding protagonist floats between dreams, reality and imagination. Circus acts follow on from serious conversations, dramatic situations evaporate into fancy fantasies. At one point, all the women who ever played a part in his life gather in the maestro's house—and still love him. On the one hand, Fellini's masterpiece is the bizarre comedy of a ridiculous man. On the other, it's a bleak inventory in harsh black-and-white, traversed by desperation and self-pity.

8 1/2; Italy/France 1963; D: Federico Fellini; P: Angelo Rizzoli; Sc: Ennio Flaiano, Tullio Pinelli, Federico Fellini, Brunello Rondi; DoP: Gianni Di Venanzo; Cast: Marcello Mastroianni, Claudia Cardinale, Anouk Aimée, Sandra Milo, Barbara Steele; B&W, 138 min.

Rank
49

THE LEOPARD

The days of the leopards are gone, the future is for the coyotes and the jackals, sighs Prince Don Fabrizio Salina, sublimely played by the great Burt Lancaster. Here, he gets to the heart of both Lampedusa's novel and Visconti's congenial adaptation: at the end of the 19th century, Sicily is on the brink of radical political and social changes. The old aristocracy, represented by Salina with dignity and mild patriarchal vigor, is about to lose its power. But, at this point in time, the splendor does still exist; Visconti celebrates the noble savoir vivre with majestic compositions and lush arrangements. The story, in contrast, is told in an understated, almost oblique fashion. Salina's sense for change and his own mortality are expressed by gestures and glances, not by words. He is smart enough to make a pact with the future forces—in order to ensure continuity at least for his own family.

Il gattopardo; Italy/France 1963; D: Luchino Visconti; P: Goffredo Lombardo; Sc: Suso Cecchi D'Amico, Pasquale Festa Campanile, Enrico Medioli, Massimo Franciosa, Luchino Visconti; DoP: Giuseppe Rotunno; Cast: Burt Lancaster, Claudia Cardinale, Alain Delon, Paolo Stoppa, Terence Hill; Color, 205 min. (premiere), 187 (restoration).

Rank
92

DR. STRANGELOVE OR: HOW I LEARNED TO STOP WORRYING AND LOVE THE BOMB

Earth's nuclear annihilation, precipitated by a military officer's single-handed act of lunacy immediately answered by a counterstrike of the enemy? Such a doom and gloom scenario seems to be a bit too simplistic in times of multi-

farious dangers and an ever-growing complexity in global relations. But Stanley Kubrick's hilarious, bloodcurdling satire conveys not only a precise psychogram of an era that was dominated by two opposing superpowers. It points beyond the cynical power games of the Cold War by clairvoyantly reducing the controllability of modern warfare mechanisms to absurdity with one indisputable argument: the most dangerous weapon of mass destruction is man. Peter Sellers' threefold appearance as a British officer, the US President and a mad Nazi scientist is so marvellous that the laughter that should stick in our throats blasts out like Major »King« Kong's *Yee-haw* when he sits astraddle the deadly bomb, hysterically riding towards destiny.

UK 1964; D, P: Stanley Kubrick; Sc: Stanley Kubrick, Terry Southern, Peter George; DoP: Gilbert Taylor; Cast: Peter Sellers, George C. Scott, Sterling Hayden, Keenan Wynn, Slim Pickens; B&W, 96 min.

Rank
24

PERSONA

PERSONA belongs to the group of early Bergman films that still catch us off guard with their radical nature. So, cinema used to be that brave, rigorous and headstrong? And, at the same time, so deep, truthful and complicated? The first scene shows an act of creation and, as a sideline, how the images come into this world. It is an abstract and experimental beginning that sets the agenda for an intensive duel (and duet) between two women. One, Liv Ullmann, an upper-class actress, has stopped talking right in the middle of a stage show—because of exhaustion or self-hatred, who knows. The other, Bibi Andersson, a nurse and unselfish petite bourgeoise, is supposed to give her a leg-up. Thus, one of them always listens while the other keeps chattering on and on. It is a fascinating dialog of glimpses and emotions, a game of approach and distance, healing and tormenting, analysis and therapy. The two are so different, yet so alike that their faces, caught by Sven Nykvist's wonderful camera eye, merge into one: two masks, unmasked.

Persona; Sweden 1966; D, Sc, P: Ingmar Bergman; DoP: Sven Nykvist; Cast: Bibi Andersson, Liv Ullmann, Margaretha Krook, Gunnar Björnstrand; B&W, 85 min.

Rank
93

THE GOOD, THE BAD AND THE UGLY

Leone's DOLLAR movies are cold experimental arrangements by design, cynical, abstract and artificial. They take pleasure in relocating the western genre to a European realm

of fantasy where everything is about form and structure, not about historical accuracy. In this vicinity, it's crucial how you narrow your eyes to slits before pulling the trigger; how cool you remain when the other guy is hard on your heels; how shrewd they rip each other off, these greasy, unshaven, impertinent scoundrels who want nothing but a few dollars more. The trilogy's third and most extravagant piece is set during the American Civil War and deals with a hurly-burly race between Clint Eastwood's man with no name, raptor-like Lee Van Cleef and Eli Wallach, taking great relish in his own nastiness. Before they confront each other in a memorable three-way shootout, accompanied by Ennio Morricone's musical cry of a hyena, they celebrate endless sadomasochistic rituals. They are paradoxical heroes, the most sympathetic deadly enemies you could imagine.

Il buono, il brutto, il cattivo; Italy/Spain 1966; D: Sergio Leone; P: Alberto Grimaldi; Sc: Age Incrocci, Furio Scarpelli, Sergio Leone, Luciano Vincenzoni; DoP: Tonino Delli Colli; Cast: Clint Eastwood, Eli Wallach, Lee Van Cleef. Color, 178 min.

Rank
35

BONNIE AND CLYDE

Black-and-white photographs from the Thirties, combined with the familiar click of a *Box Brownie* camera, evoke expectations of nostalgia, but, only moments later, jump cuts and other Nouvelle Vague references pull us right back into the Swinging Sixties. Arthur Penn, a director specializing in the revision of American myths, perfectly encapsulated 1967's rebellious zeitgeist in this movie. The two handsome anti-heroes of his singular gangster ballad scored big with young audiences, triggered a retro fashion trend and, above all, dealt the death blow to Hollywood's anachronistic Production Code. BONNIE AND CLYDE is especially courageous and innovative in its depiction of violence, which Penn wanted to show as realistically as possible. In the final scene, it feels like the bodies

of the legendary outlaw couple are riddled by a thousand machine gun bullets. Agonizingly long and deeply unsettling, this sequence, with its obvious references to the Kennedy assassination and the Vietnam war, ranks among the most radical images ever created by American mainstream cinema.

Bonnie and Clyde; USA 1967; D: Arthur Penn; P: Warren Beatty; Sc: David Newman, Robert Benton; DoP: Burnett Guffey; Cast: Warren Beatty, Faye Dunaway, Michael J. Pollard, Gene Hackman, Estelle Parsons; Color, 111 min.

Rank
97

2001: A SPACE ODYSSEY

During the prologue, a bone is turned into a weapon. Moments later, it gets thrown into the air and, with the help of the boldest cut in movie history, transforms into a spaceship that flies through outer space millions of years later. This is how Stanley Kubrick encapsulates technical evolution—in a both elegant and laconic fashion. On the whole, 2001 describes a circle, from the origins of human culture to their demise, from genesis to decay to new coming-into-being. In between, there are great moments: the Viennese waltz

of a round space shuttle; the daily routine of two astronauts on their way to Jupiter; the sophisticated duel between one of them and the mastermind computer HAL 9000; the psychedelic trip to infinity and beyond. It's a grand and magnificent vision, with radical jumps and discontinuities, majestic images and a groundbreaking visual style. It can also be considered as a kind of »anti-STAR WARS«: science fiction without an ostensible plot, free of the banal conflict between good and evil. Instead, it deals, in its own solemn rhythm, with substantial philosophic questions. And remains a mystery that can never be unraveled completely.

2001: A Space Odyssey; UK/USA 1968; D, P: Stanley Kubrick; Sc: Stanley Kubrick, Arthur C. Clarke; DoP: Geoffrey Unsworth; Cast: Keir Dullea, Gary Lockwood, William Sylvester, Daniel Richter, Leonard Rossiter; Color, 149 min.

Rank
3

ONCE UPON A TIME IN THE WEST

From the near-silent first sequence at the railroad station to the final showdown between Charles Bronson and Henry Fonda, all the typical elements are there: the way to the West; a young and chaotic civilization seeking order; the picturesque mountains of Ford's Monument Valley; a revenge

story about a man living only for the moment of retaliation. Still, ONCE UPON A TIME IN THE WEST transcends the genre like no other western in movie history. Sergio Leone's direction is all about

form and style, with every image a carefully composed painting, every face a characteristic landscape, every shootout a perfectly orchestrated ballet, every musical motive an unforgettable hymn. Leone, quoting the American classics as well as his own DOLLAR westerns, creates a total artwork of rare majesty, the most beautiful and deep of the late westerns.

C'era una volta il West; Italy/USA 1968; D: Sergio Leone; P: Fulvio Morsella; Sc: Sergio Leone, Sergio Donati; DoP: Tonino Delli Colli; Cast: Claudia Cardinale, Henry Fonda, Jason Robards, Charles Bronson, Gabriele Ferzetti; Color, 165 min.

ANDREI RUBLEV

Tarkovsky is a unique figure in movie history. His cinema is as close to classic Russian literature as it is to Far Eastern

meditation. His style is defined by tranquility and slowness, an atmosphere heavy with meaning, spiritual murmur and a very physical, sensual grasp. Next to SOLARIS and STALKER, ANDREI RUBLEV is one of his main works, a three-hour walk through history that is more powerful and gripping than Tarkovsky's other films, but still full of riddles and secret codes. It tells the story of icon painter Rublev who wanders through medieval Rus-

sia in search of work and fulfillment, but finds brute force and primitive circumstances instead. At times, all he does is observe events that can hardly be described as a narrative in the traditional sense. It is more like a rough draft: archaic sketches of religion, art and politics that are never completely within one's reach.

Andrei Rublev; USSR 1969; D: Andrei Tarkovsky; P: Tamara Ogorodnikova; Sc: Andrei Konchalovsky, Andrei Tarkovsky; DoP: Vadim Yusov; Cast: Anatoly Solonitsyn, Ivan Lapikov, Nikolai Sergeyev, Irma Raush; B&W, 205 min.

Rank
74

THE WILD BUNCH

What BONNIE AND CLYDE did in 1967 for the gangster movie, THE WILD BUNCH repeated two years later for the western: the rejuvenation of a genre by an unprecedented bluntness in the depiction of violence. Especially famous are the excessive mass gun shoot-outs. Director Sam Peckinpah composed these sequences with meticulous precision from hundreds of shots and turned them into strangely gripping, bloody choreographies of killing. The devastating impact of bullets has seldom been demonstrated to greater effect. The eponymous »wild bunch« is a rowdy gang of bandits headed by a grizzled outlaw (William Holden). In 1913—at a time when the »Wild West« had already ceased to exist—, they decide to try one last big raid. Chased by bounty hunters and

caught between the fronts of the Mexican Revolution, these men know that they have lived past their time. Instead of waiting for the end, they proudly ride towards their destiny, without regret, committed only to their own peculiar code of honor. For all its ruggedness and brutality, in these moments the film also manages to be an elegiac farewell to an era that is irrevocably lost.

The Wild Bunch; USA 1969; D: Sam Peckinpah; P: Phil Feldman; Sc: Walon Green, Sam Peckinpah; DoP: Lucien Ballard; Cast: William Holden, Ernest Borgnine, Robert Ryan, Edmond O'Brien, Warren Oates; Color, 134 min. / 145 min. (Director's Cut).

Rank
53

A CLOCKWORK ORANGE

The world is a cold, sterile and morally depraved place in this chilling futuristic vision. We follow Alex (Malcolm McDowell), the charismatic leader of a gang of juvenile delinquents, on his way from being an unscrupulous sociopath to ending up a brainwashed yea-sayer whose stomach turns at the mere thought of violence. For his adaptation of Anthony Burgess' social satire, Kubrick developed an extraordinary visual language that combines extreme wide-angle shots, strict symmetries and painstaking choreographies in a most effective way. The soundtrack bolsters this »horrorshow« with synthesizer sounds and excerpts of Beethoven and

 Rossini, doing its bit to make the viewer's hair stand on end. For many, Kubrick's aestheticization of extreme acts of violence went too far. Scenes such as Alex raping a woman and maiming her husband for life while lilting *Singin' in the Rain* led to the film being banned in British movie theaters for decades. Whatever view one has about this, at the end of the day, the question remains whether murderers, too, have a right to a free will. An eery masterpiece by one of cinema's most audacious innovators.

A Clockwork Orange; UK 1971; D, P, Sc: Stanley Kubrick; DoP: John Alcott; Cast: Malcolm McDowell, Patrick Magee, Michael Bates, Warren Clarke, Adrienne Corri; Color, 136 min.

Rank
25

THE GODFATHER

»I believe in America«, Bonasera, the undertaker, solemnly declares in the first shot. But the three-hour mafia epic that follows lays to rest the myth of the *Land of the Free*.

The American pursuit of hegemony is interpreted as a modern version of the bloody feuds of Italian nobility. Don Vito, the formidable patriarch of the Corleone clan, exudes noblesse, tradition and dignity with every ponderous gesture, each melancholic glance and knowing sigh. Illegal dealings, family celebrations, assassinations—everything is strictly ritualized in organized crime's high society. Power struggles, betrayal and revenge are the driving forces behind a deadly cycle of violence and more violence. With fateful irreversibility, the murderous events unfold in somber, ominous images, accompanied by Nino Rota's mournful score. Everything culminates in the final parallel montage when Michael Corleone's new title of godfather assumes a double meaning as he gets rid of all of his enemies in a merciless act of retribution. A gem of a movie that raised Francis Ford Coppola to the ranks of great directors, gave Marlon Brando a well-deserved comeback, and made the virtually unknown Al Pacino a global celebrity.

The Godfather; USA 1972; D: Francis Ford Coppola; P: Albert S. Ruddy; Sc: Mario Puzo, Francis Ford Coppola; DoP: Gordon Willis; Cast: Marlon Brando, Al Pacino, James Caan, Robert Duvall, Diane Keaton; Color, 175 min.

Rank
2

AGUIRRE, THE WRATH OF GOD

In the multi-faceted oeuvre of Werner Herzog, his collaborations with Klaus Kinski rank among the most famous and highly praised. Like no other, the fearless filmmaker managed to extract extraordinary performances from the

outrageous actor and enfant terrible of German cinema, as this, their first encounter, proves. Kinski charges his character with a feverish energy that keeps the film afloat like the rafts of the conquistadores on the Amazon river during their doomed search for the legendary El Dorado. Even more important are the atmospheric images which Herzog and his small team shot in a hazardous fashion on location in Peru. When the sizeable group of explorers descends from the fogbound heights of the Andes to the sound of Popol Vuh's mysterious music, AGUIRRE instantly unfolds a magical realism that is mesmerizing. Herzog forgoes the panoramic views typical of the genre in favor of close and narrow shots, making the viewer feel like an eyewitness of real events. Don Lope de Aguirre's final address to a horde of monkeys is only one of many scenes that influenced Coppola's APOCALYPSE NOW: »I am the wrath of God. Who else is with me?«

Aguirre, der Zorn Gottes; West Germany 1972; D, Sc: Werner Herzog; P: Werner Herzog, Hans Prescher; DoP: Thomas Mauch; Cast: Klaus Kinski, Helena Rojo, Del Negro, Ruy Guerra, Peter Berling; Color, 93 min.

Rank
90

CHINATOWN

In CHINATOWN, 1930's Los Angeles is a sophisticated and classy place. But beneath the surface of this idyllic world lurk corruption and treason, violence and abuse. Private eye J.J. Gittes, played by Jack Nicholson with a sublime blend of machismo and reflectiveness, looks below the surface for a living. At the outset, it appears to be a small case—as it always does. But the alleged extra-marital affair is only a side issue of a fully-fledged city scandal and a family tragedy of Shakespearian proportions. Author Robert Towne elegantly intertwines elements of L.A.'s history and the patterns of the hard-boiled detective genre. The characters are drawn so beautifully and the plot is wo-

ven so skillfully that his script is still a shining example of the art of screenwriting. Roman Polanski's direction, on the other hand, is of almost painful precision, at no time is there any doubt that the events are relentlessly heading for disaster. It was only during the heyday of New Hollywood that American mainstream cinema was so radical, complex and daring.

Chinatown; USA 1974; D: Roman Polanski; P: Robert Evans; Sc: Robert Towne; DoP: John A. Alonzo; Cast: Jack Nicholson, Faye Dunaway, John Huston, Perry Lopez, John Hillerman; Color, 131 min.

Rank
11

THE GODFATHER: PART II

With an elaborate structure, Coppola extends the Corleone saga historically and geographically, letting it span half a century and reach from California to Cuba, with a side trip to Sicily squeezed into the bargain. Alternating between two storylines, the film describes Don Michael's expansion efforts in the 1950s as well as the beginnings of his father Vito, who immigrates to the USA in 1901 as an orphan child, raises a family in New York and lays the foundation of his later empire by committing a cold-blooded murder. For Vito, the determination to protect his family by all necessary means may be rooted in the terrible experiences of his childhood. But for his increasingly emotionless son, the same promise merely serves as an excuse to justify a megalomania that stops at nothing, not even at a fratricide. In spite of its epic length, the second instalment in Coppola's mafia trilogy is a prime example of filmic elegance and narrational economy. Quintessential American cinema.

The Godfather: Part II; USA 1974; D, P: Francis Ford Coppola; Sc: Francis Ford Coppola, Mario Puzo; DoP: Gordon Willis; Cast: Al Pacino, Robert De Niro, Robert Duvall, Diane Keaton, John Cazale; Color, 200 min.

Rank
15

NASHVILLE

In their best moments, Robert Altman's movies resemble life itself in that they are unstructured, meandering, sometimes meaningless, full of surprises and always in a state of flux. NASHVILLE is the most accomplished example of his unique ability to generate realism by accumulating seemingly random scenes and casually overheard conversations. Without following a stringent plot, the movie takes an unflattering look at the artificial showbiz world shaping the life of country music's capital. About two dozen characters encounter each other in changing constellations, pushing forward into the spotlight, permanently looking for recognition, a record deal or just another affair.  Also competing for attention is an independent presidential candidate whose unconventional slogans resound from speakers all over town. When a bloody incident occurs on a big party event, this ugly fissure in the idyllic country world is covered up instantly. Altman has created a filmic and musical kaleidoscope that reveals a sad America on the eve of its bicentennial. A nation that, traumatized by Vietnam and Watergate, keeps its eyes shut, afraid to face reality and sink into depression.

Nashville; USA 1975; D, P: Robert Altman; Sc: Joan Tewkesbury; DoP: Paul Lohmann; Cast: Henry Gibson, Ronee Blakley, Lily Tomlin, Keith Carradine, Geraldine Chaplin; Color, 159 min.

Rank
69

JAWS

Compared with his descendants, the first blockbuster which was actually referred to as such is a downright subtle achievement. But while it brought a new formula to Hollywood's business model (huge budget + enormous marketing force = gigantic profit), at its heart, it still pays homage to classical genre cinema and demonstrates the power of old school sto-

rytelling. From the pre-title sequence's initial shark attack (accompanied by John Williams' unforgettable score) to the explosive conclusion on the high sea, Spielberg's direction builds tension in the mould of a Hitchcock thriller. He keeps the audience on the edge of their seats by creating a clever blend of suspense, shock and comic relief. It's wonderful how he takes his sweet time to characterize the three men who sooner or later will need a bigger boat. We know them really well when the shark surfaces for the first time—at a point when the common monster movie's titles are already rolling: after 76 whole minutes.

Jaws; USA 1975; D: Steven Spielberg; P: David Brown, Richard D. Zanuck; Sc: Peter Benchley, Carl Gottlieb; DoP: Bill Butler; Cast: Roy Scheider, Robert Shaw, Richard Dreyfuss, Lorraine Gary, Murray Hamilton; Color, 124 min.

Rank
22

ONE FLEW OVER THE CUCKOO'S NEST

Gambler and fake, democrat and maverick, bohemian and revolutionary: this R.P. McMurphy, portrayed divinely by Jack Nicholson, is one truly great character from the seventies. With 1968, the Vietnam War and Watergate still in the air, he rebels against the establishment and cocks a snook at the system. To avoid prison, he has himself committed to a mental institution full of dozing inmates and frosty nurses, throwing the place into turmoil in no time. McMurphy confronts the institute's

depressing routine with libertarian vitality and wicked humor; audiences loved him for that and so did the Academy, awarding Milos Forman's powerful masterpiece with five main Oscars, one for Nicholson as best actor. Still, the protagonist is not granted a victory against the ruling class. He fails because the authorities are too strong while he has his obvious weaknesses. Despite his merits, above all, he's still a sophomoric small-time crook.

One Flew Over the Cuckoo's Nest; USA 1975; D: Milos Forman; P: Michael Douglas, Saul Zaentz; Sc: Bo Goldman, Lawrence Hauben; DoP: Haskell Wexler; Cast: Jack Nicholson, Louise Fletcher, Danny DeVito, Christopher Lloyd, Brad Dourif; Color, 133 min.

Rank
33

TAXI DRIVER

As the taxi cab glides elegantly over the tarmac, accompanied by Bernard Herrmann's sometimes wistful, sometimes menacing soundtrack, it is the perfect metaphor for the lonely drifter: sealed off, incapable of connecting to the outside world, aimless but always on the move. Unaffected, it dives through spouts of water; fearless, it cuts through screens of fog, its metallic skin reflecting the neon messages of nighttime New York. Sitting at its wheel is a human time bomb inexorably ticking away towards its detonation, a Vietnam veteran unable to end the war inside him. He talks to his mirror image, writes apocalyptic visions into his diary and

carries out ritual acts in order to prepare himself for a bloodbath that is supposed to cleanse him. But even after the gates of mayhem open wide, the longed-for catharsis never comes. The triumvirate Schrader, Scorsese and De Niro found its common thread—male fantasies, male obsessions, male violence—and together created Travis Bickle, one of the most unforgettable characters of film history: God's lonely man.

Taxi Driver; USA 1976; D: Martin Scorsese; P: Michael Phillips, Julia Phillips; Sc: Paul Schrader; DoP: Michael Chapman; Cast: Robert De Niro, Jodie Foster, Cybill Shepherd, Peter Boyle, Albert Brooks; Color, 113 min.

Rank
7

ANNIE HALL

Measured against his only genuine triumph at the Academy Awards (among others, Best Picture and Best Original Screenplay), Woody Allen's previous efforts look like silly banter. ANNIE HALL is the big leap that turned a brilliant jester into an inspired filmmaker. With great virtuosity, this romantic comedy switches between different levels of time and place, reality and fantasy, while comedy writer Alvy Singer (Allen) recounts his  tragicomic relationship with the aspiring songstress Annie Hall (Diane Keaton). Directly addressing the audience, Alvy reveals all the agonizing details of their ill-fated romance: from the first, awkward flirt to their problems at having sex (she can only do it when she's stoned), to the horrific Easter visit to Annie's deeply Anglo-Saxon Protestant family; from the disastrous trips to Los Angeles, which initiate and cement their break-up, to their accidental and friendly re-encounter in a New York café. All of this happens in a spellbinding combination of tender melancholia, farcical sitcom, sharp one-liners and graceful images, garnished with shrink jokes, egghead mockery, cheerful self-depreciation and caustic skits against Hollywood's entertainment industry. This is Allen's CITIZEN KANE.

Annie Hall; USA 1977; D: Woody Allen; P: Charles H. Joffe; Sc: Woody Allen, Marshall Brickman; DoP: Gordon Willis; Cast: Woody Allen, Diane Keaton, Tony Roberts, Carol Kane, Paul Simon; Color, 93 min.

Rank
39

STAR WARS

Looking back at the reception of many a movie classic, it is obvious that a large number of masterpieces initially were either critical failures or box office bombs. Or both. Looking at the blockbusters, though, it is amazing how many

of them either suffered from rough production circumstances or from a lack of self-confidence on the side of their makers. Or both. In 1977, Hollywood did not have much faith in George Lucas and his strange war of the stars, a project that blended elements from westerns, war movies, adventure movies *and* knight movies with the science fiction genre. It was not until it skyrocketed at its theatrical release that its unbelievable force became apparent. The rest, as they say, is history. STAR WARS was an incredible mainstream success around the globe. It hit a pop culture nerve, invented the term of 'merchandising' for Hollywood's vocabulary and launched a new brand with countless sequels, prequels and spin-offs. But is it a perfect film? Not exactly. Rather, it is a perfect event, with unforgettable characters, amazing scenes and brilliant effects—a magical trip to another galaxy.

Star Wars; USA 1977; D, Sc: George Lucas; P: Gary Kurtz; DoP: Gilbert Taylor; Cast: Mark Hamill, Harrison Ford, Carrie Fisher, Peter Cushing, Alec Guinness; Color, 121 min.

Rank
19

THE DEER HUNTER

The most memorable scene, and the dramatic heart of the movie, is the forced Russian roulette duel between the two soldiers played by Robert De Niro and Christopher Walken.

The nerve-wracking tension culminates in an act of liberation when they finally turn their guns against their Vietnamese tormentors. After that, there's no turning back. Forever gone are the innocence and recklessness that Michael Cimino celebrates during the long exposition. The repatri-

ates are wounded physically and mentally. All that awaits them at home is a bleak feeling of alienation. THE DEER HUNTER, a masterpiece of cinematic realism, is less a war movie than a study of internal and external changes caused by war. Meticulously, Cimino portrays the microcosm of the steel worker town of Clairton, Pennsylvania—at the same time making tangible the American Vietnam trauma with all its emotional force.

The Deer Hunter; USA 1978; D: Michael Cimino; P: Michael Cimino, Michael Deeley, John Peverall, Barry Spikings; Sc: Deric Washburn; DoP: Vilmos Zsigmond; Cast: Robert De Niro, Christopher Walken, Meryl Streep, John Cazale, John Savage; Color, 182 min.

Rank
78

APOCALYPSE NOW

»My film«, Francis Ford Coppola once said, »is not about Vietnam. It *is* Vietnam.« The mother of all (anti-)war movies is a truly singular experience. In a creative and directorial tour de force, Coppola took John Milius's Conrad adapta-

tion and forged it into a phantasmagoria of a trip to hell. In all its hubris, this unparalleled material battle could be the late apex of the »old«, analog cinema. Watching it in the digital age, it feels strange to realize that everything seen on screen is actually there— helicopter formations, napalm explosions, whole armies of extras, even the tiger in the jungle. Inventing psychedelic hallucinations, horrifying acts of violence and archaic, primal images, the film presses forward, deeper and deeper into the heart of darkness, finally arriving at a place devoid of all civilization, moral, reason, or hope. It is the place where »the horror« waits. In his most sinister role, Marlon Brando portrays a man who has delved into the deepest recesses of his soul and lost his mind on the way. A brave and truthful work of art.

Apocalypse Now; USA 1979; D, P: Francis Ford Coppola; Sc: John Milius, Francis Ford Coppola; DoP: Vittorio Storaro; Cast: Marlon Brando, Martin Sheen, Robert Duvall, Frederic Forrest, Sam Bottoms; Color, 153 min. / 202 min. (REDUX Version).

Rank
5

ALIEN

ALIEN is all about teamwork. For a start, there's the crew of seven astronauts on board of the Nostromo, fighting what's probably the most persistent and long-living alien in science fiction cinema history. It's only in the end that Sigourney Weaver crystal-  lizes as the journey's only survivor. On the other hand, there's the crew behind the camera, creating a true designer marvel, from the spaceship's nightmarish maze through

 H.R. Giger's metallic, dripping-wet creatures to a filmic look that even today feels innovative and futuristic. Director Ridley Scott, reveling in beauty, allows enough time to establish characters and settings—making the subsequent shocks all the more effective. The alien's »birth« and the android's exposure are only two of the unforgettable thrills of this chilling horror trip.

Alien; UK 1979; D: Ridley Scott; P: Gordon Carroll, David Giler, Walter Hill; Sc: Dan O'Bannon; DoP: Derek Vanlint; Cast: Sigourney Weaver, Tom Skerrit, Ian Holm, John Hurt, Harry Dean Stanton; Color, 117 min.

Rank
30

THE EMPIRE STRIKES BACK

The first sequel to George Lucas's cross-generational pop fairy tale deserves its place in this book, too, since it contains some of the greatest STAR WARS moments of all. Suf-

fused by Far Eastern wisdom, Luke's apprenticeship with his cuddlesome, but wise mentor Yoda is a welcome emotional island in a sweeping stream of technically perfect action sequences. Leia's vow of love to Han Solo and his heroic re-action, only moments before being deep-frozen, lift their romance to a cosmic level. And Darth Vader's confession that he is Luke's father transforms the audience into a state of shock of galactic proportions.

By hiring three well-versed professionals for script (Leigh Brackett and Lawrence Kasdan) and direction (Irvin Kershner), »Big George« kept the force of mythical storytelling on his side. EMPIRE carries forward the intriguing inventiveness of its predecessor and already hints at the ultimate triumph of good over evil which is consummated in the next episode—a long time ago in a galaxy far, far away ...

Star Wars: Episode V: The Empire Strikes Back; USA 1980; D: Irvin Kershner; P: Gary Kurtz; Sc: Leigh Brackett, Lawrence Kasdan; DoP: Peter Suschitzky; Cast: Mark Hamill, Harrison Ford, Carrie Fisher, Billy Dee Williams, David Prowse; Color, 124 min. / 127 min. (Special Edition).

Rank
56

THE SHINING

The Overlook Hotel may be situated in Colorado, but for some of its visitors, the rules of The Eagle's *Hotel California* apply: you can check-out any time you like, but you can never leave! Jack Torrance (Jack Nicholson in his most furious role), caretaker for the winter, wannabe-writer and lousy husband, is such a guest. As an eternal revenant, he seems to be damned to execute the same work—and the same bloody murders—over and over again. There's a symbiotic link between Jack and the haunted house—the limits of time and space don't matter in their relationship. Stanley Kubrick is right when refusing us any kind of certainty; in its

maze-like, symmetrical, multi-layered system, the film hides more than it reveals. At the same time, on the psychological level, THE SHINING is quite straightforward. Subtract the fantastic element and all that remains is a sad family drama in which cracks turn into breaches, in which violence grows out of estrangement.

The Shining; UK/USA 1980; D, P: Stanley Kubrick; Sc: Stanley Kubrick, Diane Johnson; DoP: John Alcott; Cast: Jack Nicholson, Shelley Duvall, Danny Lloyd, Scatman Crothers, Joe Turkel; Color, 146 min. / 119 min. (European Version).

Rank
71

RAGING BULL

Like many of his great films, Martin Scorsese's probably most personal work is an honest examination of machismo and male violence. RAGING BULL is based on the autobiog-

raphy of New York native Jake LaMotta, a middleweight boxer who fought his way from the gyms of the Bronx to the title of world champion. On his journey to the top, Scorsese's LaMotta destroys everything he loves, unable to control instincts and emotions that dominate him more than his opponents in the ring ever could. Robert De Niro, awarded with a richly deserved Oscar, acts like a champion, boxes like a professional and put on more than fifty pounds in order to be able to portray the aged LaMotta convincingly. The overweight ex-champion ends up deserted by his family and friends. Lonely, frustrated and lusting after underage girls, he is still convinced of being a big shot, reassuring himself in the mirror that he is »the boss«. Scorsese and his fabulous editor Thelma Schoonmaker created the spectacular fight sequences so violently and close to the action that they inevitably make the viewer flinch with every blow. A knockout.

Raging Bull; USA 1980; D: Martin Scorsese; P: Robert Chartoff, Irwin Winkler; Sc: Paul Schrader, Mardik Martin; DoP: Michael Chapman; Cast: Robert De Niro, Cathy Moriarty, Joe Pesci, Frank Vincent, Nicholas Colasanto; B&W/Color, 129 min.

Rank
18

RAIDERS OF THE LOST ARK

Steven Spielberg had always dreamt of making a James Bond film. George Lucas suggested to him that they team up and invent something even better. The duo eventually came up with a wonderfully old-fashioned adventure movie in the style of the comics and dime novels they had so enthusiastically consumed in their childhood. Set in the 1930s, it is spiked with secrets and dangers, mysteries and mean villains, a beautiful girl and a larger-than-life hero. With his famous fedora and bullwhip, Harrison Ford transforms himself into a modern-day Humphrey Bogart and will always be re-

membered as the fearless archeologist Professor Jones. Similar to STAR WARS, the Indiana Jones series generously avails itself of tried and tested myths and patterns, presenting a world neatly divided into good and evil. For all the spectacle, the breathtaking stunts and special effects, Spielberg and Lucas always remember to blend in a pinch of humor. Indestructible movie entertainment, as stone washed as Indy's leather jacket.

Raiders of the Lost Ark; USA 1981; D: Steven Spielberg; P: Frank Marshall; Sc: Lawrence Kasdan; DoP: Douglas Slocombe; Cast: Harrison Ford, Karen Allen, Paul Freeman, John Rhys-Davies, Ronald Lacey; Color, 115 min.

Rank
48

E.T. THE EXTRA-TERRESTRIAL

One critic suggested that E.T. is the best Disney movie never produced by Disney. Another one felt the alien was way too cuddly: essentially, it's more like a dog and E.T., a Lassie movie in disguise. Both can't be denied. After all, Steven Spielberg's mega-blockbuster deliberately follows the rules of classic family entertainment, telling the tale of a lonely boy and his faithful friend, an all too familiar story about growing up and getting stronger. So, what does make E.T. so special? It's not the sci-fi element which got imposed on

other genres a lot during the Eighties, but the sensitive and stylish direction that blends naïvety, comedy, suspense and emotion so masterfully. Spielberg's camera almost exclusively takes the children's point of view, while the adults appear anonymous and dangerous. As a result, even those in the audience who have long since left childhood behind are turned into wondering youngsters.

E.T. the Extra-Terrestrial; USA 1982; D: Steven Spielberg; P: Steven Spielberg, Kathleen Kennedy; Sc: Melissa Mathison; DoP: Allen Daviau; Cast: Henry Thomas, Dee Wallace, Drew Barrymore, Peter Coyote, Robert MacNaughton; Color, 115/120 Min.

Rank
42

BLADE RUNNER

BLADE RUNNER is all about style. It's about architecture, wardrobe, decor, colors, light, and music. Ridley Scott is a designer at heart, he utilizes yesterday's fashion to create tomorrow's trends, he combines film noir with science fiction, he creates a new world out of neon, rain and darkness that is artificial and believable at the same time. Each frame is thoroughly com-

posed and consists of several layers; so does the story of blade runner Rick Deckard (Harrison Ford) who hits more than one wall while hunting down the runaway

replicants. In the end, he may not understand the meaning of life, but at least realizes the value of life in itself. As a result, a profoundly human plea for tolerance lies behind all the visual bombast. A mis-

understood box office failure when first released, BLADE RUNNER has long since ascended to the pantheon of futuristic cinema's undisputed masterpieces.

Blade Runner; USA 1982; D: Ridley Scott; P: Michael Deeley; Sc: Hampton Fancher, David Peoples; DoP: Jordan Cronenweth; Cast: Harrison Ford, Rutger Hauer, Sean Young, Edward James Olmos, Daryl Hannah; Color, 117 min.

Rank
4

FANNY AND ALEXANDER

Bergman's final movie for the big screen is more than a worthy conclusion of an exceptional career. It shines as both sum and reinvention, as a document of craftsmanship and a demonstration of innovative storytelling. Siblings Fanny and Al-

exander grow up in early 20th century Sweden, experiencing a family history full of fascinating characters and wondrous developments. Everything vibrates with life, drama, hatred, love, grief, frivolity, envy, warm-heartedness, and most of it we see through the eyes of the children. It's a gaping look at the richness of existence, at the lucky and unlucky twists of fate. For the cinema, a three-hour version had to suffice; more epic broadness (but not a minute too much) can be found in the five-hour cut that Bergman edited for television.

Fanny och Alexander; Sweden/France/West Germany 1982; D, Sc: Ingmar Bergman; P: Jörn Donner; DoP: Sven Nykvist; Cast: Bertil Guve, Pernilla Allwin, Börje Ahlstedt, Allan Edwall, Ewa Fröling; Color, 188 min., 312 (director's cut).

Rank
95

ONCE UPON A TIME IN AMERICA

The phone rings endlessly, it rings from the past, from the depth of the subconsciousness, and it doesn't even stop when somebody picks up the receiver. Has there ever been a call more severe, more guilt-ridden? Sergio Leone begins his grandiose gangster epic on a mysterious note, only hesitantly revealing the order of the different time levels. The actual coherence of all this— the snotty adolescence set in lively New York City during the Twenties, the hard-boiled power struggle during the era of  Prohibition, the resolution in the strangely surreal Sixties— will only be made clear four lush and detailed hours later. It is then that the colorful biography of Robert De Niro's Jewish mobster proves to be a grievous delusion. The balance of this life characterized by violence and cruelty, frequently against women, is so devastating that it is bearable only in a delirious state. But even in a Chinese opium den, the phone keeps ringing.

Once Upon a Time in America; Italy/USA 1984; D: Sergio Leone; P: Arnon Milchan; Sc: Sergio Leone, Leonardo Benvenuti, Piero De Bernardi, Enrico Medioli, Franco Arcalli, Franco Ferrini; DoP: Tonino Delli Colli; Cast: Robert De Niro, James Woods, Elizabeth McGovern, Joe Pesci, Tuesday Weld; Color, 229 min.

BACK TO THE FUTURE

Since the release of BACK TO THE FUTURE, we have travelled almost as many years into the future as Marty McFly travelled into the past in the movie. That's more than enough for the whole inventory of this perfect entertainment machine to become pop culture classics: eccentric Doc Brown with his bulging eyes and crazy hairdo. Bulky Biff, rudely knocking and asking if there's anybody home. The spacy DeLorean, without question the coolest time machine of, well, all

times. And Marty himself of course, the hero of the last minute, the master of skateboarding, the lord of thunder, lightning and electric guitar. The fans are still brooding over the plot's logical bloopers, over the paradoxes of a story that constantly keeps defining and redefining the worlds of 1955 and 1985. But even if not all time leaps work out perfectly, BACK TO THE FUTURE is, first and foremost, an example of sheer screenwriting perfection by Bob Gale and Robert Zemeckis. The search of lost time runs like a golden thread through Zemeckis' filmography.

Back to the Future; USA 1985; D: Robert Zemeckis; P: Michael Deeley; Sc: Robert Zemeckis, Bob Gale; DoP: Dean Cundey; Cast: Michael J. Fox, Christopher Lloyd, Lea Thompson, Crispin Glover, Thomas F. Wilson; Color, 116 min.

Rank
63

BLUE VELVET

Bright yellow tulips and a white picket fence under a clear blue sky: the first shot has become a vivid part of pop culture memory; em-

blematically, it stands for the idyllic, innocent world that the film craves and, at the same time, reveals as a beautiful illusion. David Lynch's camera literally advances into the under-ground, plunging into a strange universe of crime, corruption and violence together with its adventur-ous protagonist (Kyle Mac-Lachlan). Like the young man, we are fascinated by what he encounters: a pret-ty and enigmatic woman (Isabella Rossellini), sweet music, and lots of unusu-al thrills. BLUE VELVET is easier to grasp than most other Lynch movies, but is

still all about surreal tone, a maze-like story and secrets and mysteries that can never be fully unraveled.

Blue Velvet; USA 1986; D, Sc: David Lynch; P: Richard Roth; DoP: Frederick Elmes; Cast: Kyle MacLachlan, Laura Dern, Isabella Rossellini, Dennis Hopper, Dean Stockwell; Color, 120 min.

Rank
75

DIE HARD

»So that's what it was? A fucking robbery?« the bruised and battered hero asks before the final showdown. No, there is more at stake here, even though the alleged terrorists turn

out to be simple robbers in the end. DIE HARD raises the bar on many levels. For starters, it is an impressively well-made, adrenaline-pumping action movie that keeps escalating with every plot twist before it literally blows its own roof off. It is also a classic yet unconventional western ballad about an old-school law-and-order man going it alone against a gang of cold-blooded killers. But, principally, it is a prototype for the modern franchise cinema that has come to dominate the market in recent decades with no shortage of sequels and prequels in sight. Apart from a few minor flaws owed to production circumstances, everything fits perfectly here. The narrative flow never falters, every storyline is wrapped up neatly at the end. But the crucial spark that ignites the carefully balanced fireworks of the movie is the physical presence of its leading man. Only number six on the casting list, Bruce Willis rose to the occasion and grabbed his place in action movie history.

Die Hard; USA 1988; D: John McTiernan; P: Lawrence Gordon, Joel Silver; Sc: Jeb Stuart, Steven E. de Souza; DoP: Jan de Bont; Cast: Bruce Willis, Bonnie Bedelia, Alan Rickman, Reginald VelJohnson, Paul Gleason; Color, 131 min.

Rank
98

GOODFELLAS

We are very familiar with the basic story pattern: at the movies, the average criminal career usually starts with an unstoppable rise and ends with an agonizing fall. But with Martin Scorsese, the devil is in the details. In this regard, the film doesn't care about basic rules or nice taste. It is as violent, brutal, funny, crazy, unpredictable, quick-witted, ruthless and vivid as the mobsters it depicts. For Scorsese, New York's Mafia is both a fascinating and terrifying microcosm and a very cruel enterprise. His direction is relentless, it all starts at headspinning pace and then just keeps going, while still finding the time for surprising little detours. Michael Ballhaus' cinematography, using spectacalur steadycam

shots, and the cast rank among the best that have ever been seen within the same movie. Next to Robert De Niro, who's never been more unpredictable, and Joe Pesci, who scares the living daylights out of everybody, Ray Liotta shines in the role of a lifetime.

GoodFellas; USA 1990; D: Martin Scorsese; P: Irwin Winkler; Sc: Nicholas Pileggi, Martin Scorsese; DoP: Michael Ballhaus; Cast: Ray Liotta, Robert De Niro, Joe Pesci, Lorraine Bracco, Paul Sorvino; Color, 145 min.

Rank
26

THE SILENCE OF THE LAMBS

With FBI student Clarice Starling's eyes, we look into the abyss of human existence: seldom, if ever, has a director made use of the subjective camera so radically and evidently as Jonathan Demme in this serial killer thriller. Thus, we are constantly on a par with this insecure, yet strong woman (Jodie Foster) when she advances into the prison of cultivated barbarian Hannibal Lecter (Anthony Hopkins), into the bleak

neighborhood of the killed victim, and finally into the white trash hell of psychotic Buffalo Bill (Ted Levine). The alliance between the young cop and her ambiguous mentor, probably movie history's most charismatic mass murderer of all time, develops into a sophisticated game of give and take, fear and fascination, force and fondness. The film fiddles with stereotypes, blurring the line between good and evil, power and weakness. En passant, it also creates a feministic subtext by showing the heroine as an object of the male eye and as a potential victim again and again.

The Silence of the Lambs; USA 1991; D: Jonathan Demme; P: Ron Bozman, Kenneth Utt, Edward Saxon; Sc: Ted Tally; DoP: Tak Fujimoto; Cast: Jodie Foster, Anthony Hopkins, Scott Glenn, Anthony Heald, Ted Levine; Color, 118 min.

Rank
67

TERMINATOR 2 – JUDGMENT DAY

The second TERMINATOR is actually more of a remake than a sequel. James Cameron, first and foremost, takes advantage of the opportunity to direct the glorious elements of the original again, only bigger, more expensively and spectacularly. Nevertheless, even the connoisseur can never feel safe. Every time the story is in danger of becoming too repetitive, it surprises with another flash of genius or a sophisticated diffraction of the space-time continuum. Part of that is, of course, the backflip of Schwarzenegger's human machine, not to mention the shape-shifting qualities of Robert Patrick's icy follow-up model. In part one, metal was already the secret protagonist; here, it definitely takes center stage when the killer, consisting of smooth, wonderfully radiant liquid-metal, brings morphing along from the future.

Terminator 2: Judgment Day; USA/France 1991; D, P: James Cameron; B: James Cameron, William Wisher Jr.; DoP: Adam Greenberg; Cast: Arnold Schwarzenegger, Linda Hamilton, Edward Furlong, Robert Patrick, Joe Morton; Color, 137 min.

RESERVOIR DOGS

Their suits are as black as their souls, but they have colorful names, and the crisp white of their shirts soon turns into a bloody red. After a jewel heist gone disastrously wrong, the surviving thugs assemble in an abandoned warehouse,

licking their wounds and, suspecting a traitor in their midst, lunge at each other's throats like wild and desperate animals. RESERVOIR DOGS is a stupendous debut, almost as groundbreaking and influential as BREATHLESS or MEAN STREETS, two movies also devoted to criminals and their fatal mistakes. Like Godard and Scorsese before him, Quentin Tarantino generously borrows from film history for the 1.0 version of his post-modern pop cinema, but, at the same time, he demonstrates an unmistakable, truly original voice. Tarantino's spirited style is nurtured by a remarkable blend of enthusiasm, hubris and real talent. With all his energy and bravado, he pulls off a near-classic and goes too far only once: during the torture scene, which is hard to stomach even today, many a visitor left the theater in protest.

Reservoir Dogs; USA 1992; D, Sc: Quentin Tarantino; P: Lawrence Bender; DoP: Andrzej Sekula; Cast: Harvey Keitel, Tim Roth, Michael Madsen, Chris Penn, Steve Buscemi; Color, 99 min.

Rank

SCHINDLER'S LIST

Images of indescribable cruelty, images of agonizing pain: no other motion picture has depicted World War II Nazi crime as nightmarish; seldom, if ever, has the Jewish people's suffering been described more movingly. In the thick of it: a glimmer of hope in the shape of enamel manufacturer Oskar Schindler (Liam Neeson), starting out as a member of the NSDAP party and war profiteer, but eventually changing sides and saving the lives of more than a thousand Jews. Steven Spielberg tells the story in sober black and white, almost as if this historic period has forfeited its right of color.

Precisely and objectively, neither going for emotional agitation nor for distancing abstraction, he portrays Schindler not as a heroic Samaritan, but as an egocentric bon vivant who, in the beginning, saves his Jewish bookkeeper Stern (Ben Kingsley) from deportation only to exploit him further. The screenplay even grants a certain ambivalence to barbaric warden Amon Goeth (Ralph Fiennes). Until the early nineties, Spielberg was considered as a kind of wunderkind, using the cinema as his toy. With SCHINDLER'S LIST, he took the gloves off— and graduated with honors.

Schindler's List; USA 1993; D: Steven Spielberg; P: Branco Lustig, Gerald R. Molen, Steven Spielberg; Sc: Steven Zaillan; DoP: Janusz Kaminski; Cast: Liam Neeson, Ben Kingsley, Ralph Fiennes, Caroline Goodall, Embeth Davidtz; B&W/Color, 195 min.

Rank
32

PULP FICTION

Full frontal violence, blood by the bucket, substance abuse, a rape and 257 mentions of the f-word are certainly not everyone's cup of tea. But when an exceptional narrative struc-ture, unforeseeable plot twists, razorsharp dialogues and an outstanding cast are added to the effrontery, it turns into an exquisite cocktail to be savored with perverse delight. PULP FICTION approaches its illustrious gathering of lowlives not with a wagging finger, but with outstretched hands, letting them experience miracles and making us marvel at so much ingenuity. In a brilliant gambit, three stories and their chronologies are mixed up in a seemingly arbitrary order that turns out to describe a perfect arc of suspense. That's why John Travolta's cool cat Vincent Vega is seen walking away contentedly in the last scene despite having been gunned down by Bruce Willis in a previous reel. Innovations such as the convoluted narrative style have since become standard features of modern film language. Equipped with immense knowledge about pop culture and an ambition to compete with the best, Quentin Tarantino administered cinema a massive adrenaline rush.

Pulp Fiction; USA 1994; D, Sc: Quentin Tarantino; P: Lawrence Bender; DoP: Andrzej Sekula; Cast: John Travolta, Samuel L. Jackson, Bruce Willis, Uma Thurman, Tim Roth; Color, 154 min. / 168 min. (Special Edition).

Rank
6

FORREST GUMP

A movie like a box of chocolates. Preciously packaged and beautifully crafted, it is simply irresistible. But afterwards, all this sweet stuff sits heavily on your stomach. What kind of a story is being told here? At first glance, it is the magical journey of a simple-minded boy from the South and the hapless love of his life. Equipped

with unexpected talents and the patent wisdoms of his mother, the eponymous hero, a combination of *Hans in Luck* and Voltaire's *Candide*, overcomes even the biggest obstacles with a smile on his face. Incidentally, he not only triggers cultural trends and inspires pop icons such as Elvis Presley and John Lennon, but also repeatedly changes the course of history. This is frequently enjoyable and sometimes even satirically brilliant. At the same time, it downplays the darker moments of recent US history into mere anecdotes and describes progressive social developments only in terms of their reconciliation with the American Dream. It is doubtful whether this arbitrary interpretation of events would have worked with any other star. Tom Hanks turns it into a home run.

Forrest Gump; USA 1994; D: Robert Zemeckis; P: Wendy Finerman, Steve Starkey, Steve Tisch; Sc: Eric Roth; DoP: Don Burgess; Cast: Tom Hanks, Robin Wright, Gary Sinise, Mykelti Williamson, Sally Field; Color/B&W, 142 min.

THE SHAWSHANK REDEMPTION

Frank Darabont's screen debut is, at once, a tribute to Hollywood's studio era and a kudo to Don Siegel's ESCAPE FROM ALCATRAZ. A faithful adaptation of a Stephen King novella, it skillfully builds on classical narrative tradition. The plot is not particularly original: a convict twice sentenced to life endures 20 years in a notorious maximum-security prison before accomplishing an impossible and spectacular escape. All the more impressive is the clarity of Darabont's vision: it elevates a simple story to an epic drama. His film is a hymn to friendship, a celebration of human strength of will, a plea for the power of hope and the belief in salvation.

This director is not afraid of using clichés—the corrupt warden, the sadistic guard, the brutal and abusive inmates, the tunnel dug in years of secret nocturnal labor—, but with these standard ingredients, he creates an astonishing emotional depth which culminates in the copiously celebrated final act. Tim Robbins and Morgan Freeman play out every nuance of their scenes without ever lapsing into cheap sentimentality.

The Shawshank Redemption; USA 1994; D, Sc: Frank Darabont; P: Niki Marvin; DoP: Roger Deakins; Cast: Tim Robbins, Morgan Freeman, Bob Gunton, William Sadler, Clancy Brown; Color, 142 min.

Rank
55

THE USUAL SUSPECTS

As audacious and loquacious as a Tarantino movie, as complex and stylish as the great noir classics, as intriguing as PSYCHO or FIGHT CLUB: surely, this brilliant heist thriller is not so much heart- than brain-warming. Thanks to screenwriter Christopher McQuarrie, its conclusion pulls the rug out from under the viewer's feet completely. His maze-like script, crafted with admirable finesse, combines a thrilling crime story full of nerve-wrecking suspense with a witty reflection about storytelling before finally culminating in a coup worthy of a magician. Although director Bryan Singer had to make do with modest means, he succeeds in embedding this dark tale in a shimmering narrative world in which the superb cast moves with equal confidence and pleasure. From the skillfully orchestrated opening sequence, you follow the story in a state of alertness, waiting for the one crucial hint that will unravel the web of mystery. While trying not to miss even the smallest thread of the densely woven plot, you never lose the uneasy feeling that, around the next bend, an even bigger secret is waiting, always just out of sight. No wonder when the Devil himself is pulling the strings.

The Usual Suspects; USA/Germany 1995; D: Bryan Singer; P: Michael McDonnell, Bryan Singer; Sc: Christopher McQuarrie; DoP: Newton Thomas Sigel; Cast: Stephen Baldwin, Gabriel Byrne, Kevin Spacey, Chazz Palminteri, Pete Postlethwaite; Color, 106 min.

Rank
99

FARGO

The Coen Brothers describe Minnesota, the home of their youth, as »Siberia with family restaurants«. That's exactly how the sparsely populated midwestern state looks like  in this movie. Roger Deakins' camera captures the endless snow plains in perfect panoramas. Equally well-composed are the characters. Nobody plays a loser better than William H. Macy; the car salesman Jerry Lundegaard who arranges his own wife's kidnapping in order to improve his desolate financial situation with the ransom collected from his father-in-law might be one of Macy's greatest achievements. Frances McDormand single-handedly restores our belief in the good of man as the big-eyed and heavily pregnant county police officer Marge Gunderson. And the strange couple of hired thugs, with Steve Buscemi as a thin-skinned neurotic and Peter Stormare as a tight-lipped brute, make a bizarre duo with an inner dynamic that could carry a whole film alone. A bloody farce develops from the encounter of these types, precisely conceived and expertly executed. A stone-cold classic, honored with two Academy Awards and the Cannes Palme d'Or.

Fargo; USA/UK 1996; D: Joel Coen; P: Ethan Coen; Sc: Joel Coen, Ethan Coen; DoP: Roger Deakins; Cast: Frances McDormand, William H. Macy, Steve Buscemi, Peter Stormare, Harve Presnell; Color, 98 min.

L.A. CONFIDENTIAL

This elegant police thriller deals with corruption and treason, ambition, lust and false fronts. His three (anti-)heroes are constantly presented in a different light, sometimes detecting the good within the bad, sometimes focusing on the vicious within the candid. The ruthless choleric (Russell Crowe) shows his weak spot, the opportunistic careerist (Guy Pearce) turns out to be a loyal colleague, and the peacocky cynic (Kevin Spacey) demonstrates unexpected integrity. These cops get into an impenetrable story maze, a hard-boiled James Ellroy world where a bloody mass-murder is only the beginning of a chain of perfidiously linked crimes. Curtis Hanson's direction refrains from us-

ing film noir clichés or genre quotations. Instead, he takes a sober look at 50's Los Angeles, an icy, but sun-drenched place filled with fascinating and ambiguous characters. The film contrasts the simple and often silly concepts of modern Hollywood with a tremendous intricacy. There is room for contradiction and irritation; and for a multi-layered crime plot that blends with a gripping background description.

L.A. Confidential; USA 1997; D: Curtis Hanson; P: Curtis Hanson, Arnon Milchan, Michael Nathanson; Sc: Brian Helgeland, Curtis Hanson; DoP: Dante Spinotti; Cast: Kevin Spacey, Russell Crowe, Guy Pearce, James Cromwell, Kim Basinger; Color, 138 min.

Rank
83

THE BIG LEBOWSKI

Their obvious and stunning craftsmanship notwithstanding, critics sometimes accuse filmmakers Joel and Ethan Coen of leaving their audience with a »feeling of emptiness«. They might have a point with THE BIG LEBOWSKI. But it is the Zen version of emptiness, a meditative state of bliss that agrees with the hero's maxim: *Take it easy, man.* The Dude (Jeff Bridges) doesn't have a job, a mission or a plan, and yet he possesses more than most of us: peace of mind. At least, until the day an Asian American mistakes him for a millionaire and urinates on his treasured rug. As the film turns into a hilarious pseudo-noir crime tale with nods to THE BIG SLEEP, it also addresses a substantial list of

subjects: bowling, Vietnam, fluxus art, nihilism, pornography, Judaism, techno pop and many more merge like Kahlúa and cream in a White Russian. The Dude and his bowling buddies struggle to make sense of a false kidnapping, a stolen car and a severed toe, all the while hoping to enter the next round-robin in the upcoming league game against a pervert named Jesus. Full of warmth, wit and wisdom, this brilliant comedy is one of those rare films that really get better with each viewing.

The Big Lebowski; USA/UK 1998; D, P, Sc: Joel Coen, Ethan Coen; DoP: Roger Deakins; Cast: Jeff Bridges, John Goodman, Julianne Moore, Steve Buscemi, David Huddleston; Color, 117 min.

Rank
64

SAVING PRIVATE RYAN

An American flag, flapping in the wind: the patriotic standard motif framing this movie seems to suggest otherwise, but this is neither an idealistic epic, nor a flaming anti-war drama. Many sacrifices are made, but you would be hard-pressed to point out even one true hero. These are soldiers merely doing their job; whether they do it unwillingly or frightened, with zeal or indifference doesn't matter in the living hell of D-Day. The unprecedented opening sequence with its incessant images of gut-spilling combat spares us no appalling detail; Janusz Kaminski's camera and the hyper-realistic sound design immediately draw us into the action. But this roaring attack on our senses is only an overture to the main story. In the mayhem of the allied forces' landing operation in Normandy, one single man is to be found and rescued from behind enemy lines. A seemingly absurd command coming from the top brass, it actually involves a certain logic, maybe even compassion, even if everybody knows that few will survive this mission impossible. Spielberg balances battles, group dynamics and the haunting conversations of the capable cast with his usual aplomb. Not exactly a feelgood movie.

Saving Private Ryan; USA 1998; D: Steven Spielberg; P: Ian Bryce, Mark Gordon, Gary Levinsohn, Steven Spielberg; Sc: Robert Rodat; DoP: Janusz Kaminski; Cast: Tom Hanks, Tom Sizemore, Edward Burns, Barry Pepper, Adam Goldberg; Color, 169 Min.

Rank
70

THE MATRIX

A philosophical action adventure; a foray into the history of pop culture; a clever treatise about dream and reality; a demonstration of style & design: rarely has science fiction cinema been more intelligent, more multilayered or more elegant than in THE MATRIX, the last great film of the 20th century. Neo (Keanu Reeves), bearing renewal as well as the uniqueness of »The One« in his name, follows the white rabbit into its hole like Alice, but his fall doesn't

lead him into wonderland, but into reality. It's a painful and shocking moment when Neo wakes up from his digital dream half an hour into the movie and realizes the truth about his former existence as a despicable human battery. He is then educated to become a virtual rebel, a fascinating (and slightly irritating) process that turns into a journey through time and space, suspending the rules of logic and gravity. The climactic shootout with the matrix's agents, a finale between pyrotechnics and martial arts, is breathtakingly furious. One of its innovative tricks—bullet time—set new special effects standards.

The Matrix; USA 1999; D, Sc: Andy & Lana Wachowski; P: Joel Silver; DoP: Bill Pope; Cast: Keanu Reeves, Laurence Fishburne, Carrie-Anne Moss, Hugo Weaving, Joe Pantoliano; Color, 136 min.

Rank
47

AMERICAN BEAUTY

This is not his beautiful house, this is not his beautiful wife: one day, Lester Burnham awakes and realizes that he has spent the last 20 years of his life in sedation. Suddenly, he sees himself for what he is: a torpid, middle-aged guy with a tedious office job and a too-perfect spouse, leading a joyless suburban life that has been drained of sex, drugs, and rock 'n' roll for a long time. His epiphany comes in the shape of a 16-year-old cheerleader, his daughter's best friend. Sensuous and perky, this girl not only fills his dreams with fifty shades of red, she makes him want to be alive again. But how? This

tragicomic satire on the American way of life at the close of the 20th century reminds us that a plastic bag caught in a gust of wind can reveal more of creation's wisdom than the most refined design object. Sam Mendes and Alan Ball have conceived a meditation on the transience of existence by means of classic Hollywood cinema. So much beauty can make us happy and melancholic at the same time. It can become the high point of our day.

American Beauty; USA 1999; D: Sam Mendes; P: Bruce Cohen, Dan Jinks; Sc: Alan Ball; DoP: Conrad L. Hall; Cast: Kevin Spacey, Annette Bening, Thora Birch, Wes Bentley, Chris Cooper; Color, 122 min.

FIGHT CLUB

David Fincher's films are full of dodges and deceptions, feints and false leads. Meticulously calculated, they create ambivalence and irritation, undermine expectations and deconstruct established narrative patterns. The viewer is not the director's confidant, more a clueless victim. Fincher's greatest

bluff begins as a GRADUATE for the Ikea generation, then morphs into a pamphlet of masculine self-empowerment before gliding down into the depths of our collective fears. Behind all this is Tyler Durden, a charismatic libertine and daredevil, maker of soap and savior of today's domesticated male. With knock-down arguments, he unhinges the numbing and monotonous white-collar existence of the nameless protagonist and turns it into a rollercoaster ride. In Tyler's bloody brave new world, fist fights become rituals of liberation, pain cures deadened souls and scars are medals of honor. But, like all utopias, it comes with a catch. The final punch line ranks among the most outrageous of all cinematic mindfucks. It leaves us with the strangely exhilarating feeling of having gotten away with a black eye.

Fight Club; USA/Germany 1999; D: David Fincher; P: Ross Grayson Bell, Ceán Chaffin, Art Linson; Sc: Jim Uhls; DoP: Jeff Cronenweth; Cast: Edward Norton, Brad Pitt, Helena Bonham Carter, Meat Loaf, Zach Grenier; Color, 139 min.

Rank
41

GLADIATOR

The historic drama genre had seen better days when Ridley Scott rubbed off its patina with a muscular epic at the turn of the millennium. Russell Crowe rides and strides through GLADIATOR's spectacular settings with the air and the body language of a designated emperor. He seems utterly invincible, in battle as in life, until the cruel machinations of his arch-rival destroy everything he lives for. Narrowly escaping death, the fallen commander only lives for revenge. In the blood-soaked arena of the Colosseum, he perfects the art of survival in breathtaking duels with other moribund combatants, waiting for his moment of truth. Between Crowe's heroic figure and its return to a better world stands a wor-

thy antagonist. Joaquin Phoenix sparkles with evil genius as the degenerate tyrant. A master of visual multilayering, Scott re-creates ancient Roman architecture and social life in stupendous detail. Similar to his Los Angeles in BLADE RUNNER, the eternal city becomes a protagonist of its own, turning an ancient world into a palpable here and now.

Gladiator; USA/UK 2000; D: Ridley Scott; P: David Franzoni, Branko Lustig, Douglas Wick; Sc: David Franzoni, John Logan, William Nicholson; DoP: John Mathieson; Cast: Russell Crowe, Joaquin Phoenix, Connie Nielsen, Oliver Reed, Richard Harris; Color, 155 min./171 min. (Extended Edition).

Rank
87

AMÉLIE

The fact that somehow everything is connected has rarely be proven more stringently (and charmingly) by a movie. Jean-Pierre Jeunet is on a paper chase in Paris; his film is

a visualization of the chaos theory, linking people to their stories, things to their owners, coincidences to their triggers, all the while insisting on the idea that even the most absurd occurrences have a deeper poetic meaning, a natural logic of the insane. With its high-speed storytelling and the uncounted number of crazy details, AMÉLIE might well be an unbearable movie if it were not

for its doe-eyed heroine (Audrey Toutou, as sorry as we feel for her, will *always* remain Amélie). Her love of adventure and her kindheartedness lend an astonishing gravity

to the playful goings-on; she represents selflessness and yearning at the same time: a dazzling postmodern fairy tale character for the new millennium.

Le fabuleux destin d'Amélie Poulain; France/Germany 2001; D: Jean-Pierre Jeunet; P: Claudie Ossard, Jean-Marc Deschamps, Arne Meerkamp van Embden; Sc: Guillaume Laurant, Jean-Pierre Jeunet; DoP: Bruno Delbonnel; Cast: Audrey Tautou, Mathieu Kassovitz, Rufus; Color, 122 min.

Rank
68

THE LORD OF THE RINGS

Everything about this Tolkien adaptation is gigantic. Conceived as a three-episode series from the start, produced on a 300 million dollar budget in one go, the complete works last nine or even eleven hours, depending on the version of your choice. In terms of quantity, it dwarfs every other movie project. Ever. Together, the three films were awarded 17 Oscars and grossed more than a billion dollars in the US alone. Uncounted are the stars on the screen, endless the armies of extras, phenomenal the special effects. No other director has more processing power than Peter Jackson; he is the master of the hard drives, the Lord of CGI: simultaneously old-fashioned and innovative, designing his plot as a classical hero's journey and creating worlds and creatures of undreamt perfection. It's a fantasy adventure for the 21st century, a popcorn fairy tale for the internet generation.

The Lord of the Rings; New Zealand/USA 2001/2002/2003; D: Peter Jackson; P: Peter Jackson, Barrie M. Osborne, Fran Walsh; Sc: Fran Walsh, Philippa Boyens, Peter Jackson; DoP: Andrew Lesnie; Cast: Elijah Wood, Sean Astin, Viggo Mortensen, Ian McKellen, Liv Tyler; Color, 178/179/201 min., 208/223/251 min. (extended versions).

Rank
40

CITY OF GOD

»If you run, the beast will get you. If you stay, the beast will eat you.« Either way, the options seem dire for Rocket, native of the City of God and the protagonist of this mov-

ie. Violence rules the favela on the outskirts of glamorous Rio de Janeiro. Here, the corrupt cops only show up when media coverage makes intervention inevitable. When the brutal drug wars finally culminate in a bloody massacre, a gang of children takes over and grabs the power, once again proving that there is no shortage of new delinquents in this lawless town. CITY OF GOD, based on the semi-autobiographical novel of Paulo Lins, transforms a desolate story into an explosion of rhythm, sound and innovative imagery. More than 200 non-professional actors fill every moment with an energy that defies the grim realities of life, even in the face of omnipresent death. Sometimes, the abundance of the acting personnel, combined with the manic pace, lessens the level of empathy for specific characters. But its driving rhythm and visual imagination—split screens, freeze-frames, jump cuts and other effects—make this film a big success.

Cidade de Deus; Brazil/France 2002; D: Fernando Meirelles, Kátia Lund; P: Andrea Barata Ribeiro, Mauricio Andrade Ramos; Sc: Bráulio Mantovani; DoP: César Charlone; Cast: Alexandre Rodrigues, Leandro Firmino da Hora, Phellipe Haagensen, Douglas Silva, Jonathan Haagensen; Color, 130 min.

Rank
88

THE DARK KNIGHT

Part two of Nolan's trilogy and definitely the highlight. The dark hero is dragged into the daylight and all he sees is chaos. The story centers on the helplessness of the au-thorities when being confront-ed with an antagonist who has no other goal but to destroy or-der. The Joker (Heath Ledger in his bizarre and grandiose last part) is *the* advocate of chaos. He doesn't care about money or wealth, but has an insatiable lust for anarchy. Against him, a man like Bruce Wayne, always sticking to rules and regula-tions, almost unavoidably has to fail. His initial triumph over the mob turns out to be a pyr-rhic victory; it is only through

this that the vacuum in Gotham's underworld which the Joker so gratefully utilizes can come into existence. In the end, Wayne has burdened himself with so much guilt that all he can do is accept the role of the scapegoat and leave. This might well have been Christopher Nolan's final state-ment: a depressing conclusion that sums up the whole fu-tility of Batman's existence.

The Dark Knight; USA/UK; D: Christopher Nolan; P: André Paulve; Sc: Jonathan Nolan, Christopher Nolan; DoP: Roger Hubert, Marc Fossard; Cast: Christian Bale, Heath Ledger, Aaron Eckhart, Michael Caine, Maggie Gyllenhaal, Gary Oldman, Morgan Freeman; Color, 152 min.

Rank
84

Top 100: The Ranking

Rank	Original Title (English Title), Country Year, Director	Page
1.	Citizen Kane, USA 1941, Orson Welles	26
2.	The Godfather, USA 1972, Francis Ford Coppola	67
3.	2001: A Space Odyssey, USA/UK 1968, Stanley Kubrick	62
4.	Blade Runner, USA/Hongkong/UK 1982, Ridley Scott	85
5.	Apocalypse Now, USA 1979, Francis Ford Coppola	78
6.	Pulp Fiction, USA 1994, Quentin Tarantino	96
7.	Taxi Driver, USA 1976, Martin Scorsese	74
8.	Some Like It Hot, USA 1959, Billy Wilder	47
9.	Casablanca, USA 1942, Michael Curtiz	28
10.	Singin' in the Rain, USA 1952, Stanley Donen/Gene Kelly	37
11.	Chinatown, USA 1974, Roman Polanski	69
12.	Vertigo, USA 1958, Alfred Hitchcock	46
13.	Psycho, USA 1960, Alfred Hitchcock	54
14.	Lawrence of Arabia, UK/USA 1962, David Lean	55
15.	The Godfather: Part II, USA 1974, Francis Ford Coppola	70
16.	Shichinin no samurai (Seven Samurai) Japan 1954, Akira Kurosawa	39
17.	Rear Window, USA 1954, Alfred Hitchcock	41
18.	Raging Bull, USA 1980, Martin Scorsese	82
19.	Star Wars, USA 1977, George Lucas	76
20.	North by Northwest, USA 1959, Alfred Hitchcock	49
21.	The Third Man, UK/USA 1949, Carol Reed	33
22.	Jaws, USA 1975, Steven Spielberg	72
23.	M, Germany 1931, Fritz Lang	19
24.	Dr. Strangelove or: How I Learned to Stop Worrying and Love the Bomb, USA/UK 1964, Stanley Kubrick	58
25.	A Clockwork Orange, UK/USA 1971, Stanley Kubrick	66
26.	GoodFellas, USA 1990, Martin Scorsese	91

27.	The Searchers, USA 1956, John Ford	43
28.	Gone with the Wind, USA 1939, Victor Fleming	25
29.	Sunset Blvd., 1950, Billy Wilder	34
30.	Alien, USA/UK 1979, Ridley Scott	79
31.	Tokyo monogatari (Tokyo Story) Japan 1953, Yasujiro Ozu	38
32.	Schindler's List, USA 1993, Steven Spielberg	95
33.	One Flew Over the Cuckoo's Nest, USA 1975, Milos Forman	73
34.	It's a Wonderful Life, USA 1946, Frank Capra	31
35.	Il buono, il brutto, il cattivo (The Good, the Bad and the Ugly), Italy/Spain/West Germany 1966, Sergio Leone	60
36.	The Wizard of Oz, USA 1939, Victor Fleming	24
37.	C'era una volta il West (Once Upon a Time in the West) Italy/USA 1968, Sergio Leone	63
38.	The Apartment, USA 1960, Billy Wilder	53
39.	Annie Hall, USA 1977, Woody Allen	75
40.	The Lord of the Rings New Zealand/USA 2001, Peter Jackson	109
41.	Fight Club, USA/Germany 1999, David Fincher	106
42.	E.T. the Extra-Terrestrial, USA 1982, Steven Spielberg	84
43.	All about Eve, USA 1950, Joseph L. Mankiewicz	36
44.	City Lights, USA 1931, Charles Chaplin	18
45.	Rashômon (Rashomon), Japan 1950, Akira Kurosawa	35
46.	Les quatre cents coups (The 400 Blows) France 1959, François Truffaut	48
47.	The Matrix USA/Australia 1999, Andy and Lana Wachowski	104
48.	Raiders of the Lost Ark, USA 1981, Steven Spielberg	83
49.	8 1/2, Italy/France 1963, Federico Fellini	56
50.	La règle du jeu (The Rules of the Game) France 1939, Jean Renoir	23

51.	À bout de souffle (Breathless)	51
	France 1960, Jean-Luc Godard	
52.	Bronenosets Potjomkin (Battleship Potemkin)	13
	USSR 1925, Sergej M. Eisenstein	
53.	The Wild Bunch, USA 1969, Sam Peckinpah	65
54.	Ladri di biciclette (Bicycle Thieves)	32
	Italy 1948, Vittorio De Sica	
55.	The Shawshank Redemption, USA 1994, Frank Darabont	98
56.	The Empire Strikes Back, USA 1980, Irvin Kershner	80
57.	Touch of Evil, USA 1958, Orson Welles	45
58.	Sunrise: A Song of Two Humans	16
	USA 1927, Friedrich Wilhelm Murnau	
59.	The General, USA 1926, Buster Keaton	14
60.	Metropolis, Germany 1927, Fritz Lang	15
61.	On the Waterfront, USA 1954, Elia Kazan	40
62.	The Night of the Hunter, USA 1955, Charles Laughton	42
63.	Back to the Future, USA 1985, Robert Zemeckis	88
64.	The Big Lebowski, USA/UK 1998, Joel and Ethan Coen	102
65.	La dolce vita, Italy/France 1960, Federico Fellini	50
66.	Modern Times, USA 1936, Charles Chaplin	20
67.	The Silence of the Lambs, USA 1991, Jonathan Demme	92
68.	Le fabuleux destin d'Amélie Poulain (Amélie)	108
	France/Germany 2001, Jean-Pierre Jeunet	
69.	Nashville, USA 1975, Robert Altman	71
70.	Saving Private Ryan, USA 1998, Steven Spielberg	103
71.	The Shining, UK/USA 1980, Stanley Kubrick	81
72.	Double Indemnity, USA 1944, Billy Wilder	29
73.	La grande illusion (Grand Illusion)	21
	France 1937, Jean Renoir	
74.	Andrei Rublev, USSR 1969, Andrei Tarkovsky	64
75.	Blue Velvet, USA 1986, David Lynch	89

76.	Det Sjunde inseglet (The Seventh Seal)	44
	Schweden 1957, Ingmar Bergman	
77.	Fargo, USA/UK 1996, Joel Coen	100
78.	The Deer Hunter, USA 1978, Michael Cimino	77
79.	American Beauty, USA 1999, Sam Mendes	105
80.	Terminator 2: Judgment Day	93
	USA/France 1991, James Cameron	
81.	The Gold Rush, USA 1925, Charles Chaplin	12
82.	Forrest Gump, USA 1994, Robert Zemeckis	97
83.	L.A. Confidential, USA 1997, Curtis Hanson	101
84.	The Dark Knight, USA/UK 2008, Christopher Nolan	111
85.	Les enfants du paradis (Children of Paradise)	30
	France 1945, Marcel Carné	
86.	La passion de Jeanne d'Arc (The Passion of Joan	17
	of Arc), France 1928, Carl Theodor Dreyer	
87.	Gladiator, USA/UK 2000, Ridley Scott	107
88.	Cidade de Deus (City of God)	110
	Brasil/France 2002, Fernando Meirelles	
89.	Bringing Up Baby, USA 1938, Howard Hawks	22
90.	Aguirre, der Zorn Gottes (Aguirre, the Wrath of God)	68
	West Germany 1972, Werner Herzog	
91.	The Maltese Falcon, USA 1941, John Huston	27
92.	Il gattopardo (The Leopard)	57
	Italy/France 1963, Luchino Visconti	
93.	Persona, Sweden 1966, Ingmar Bergman	59
94.	Reservoir Dogs, USA 1992, Quentin Tarantino	94
95.	Fanny och Aleksander (Fanny and Alexander)	86
	Sweden/France/West Germany 1982, Ingmar Bergman	
96.	L'avventura, Italy/France 1960, Michelangelo Antonioni	52
97.	Bonnie and Clyde, USA 1967, Arthur Penn	61
98.	Die Hard, USA 1988, John McTiernan	90

99. The Usual Suspects, USA/Germany 1995, Bryan Singer   99
100. Once Upon a Time in America   87
      Italy/USA 1984, Sergio Leone

Top 100 Directors

The following chart is based on the 1,088 titles from all our sources. This time, all films by a director—not only from the Top 100—were included. Please bear in mind that this ranking might look a little different had we assessed Best Directors Lists instead of Best Films Lists. The director's name is followed by the number of points all his or her films have earned. The number of his or her titles is shown in brackets.

Rank	Director (Number of listet Movies)	Points
1.	Alfred Hitchcock (9)	635
2.	Stanley Kubrick (9)	624
3.	Steven Spielberg (10)	616
4.	Francis Ford Coppola (6)	529
5.	Martin Scorsese (11)	498
6.	Billy Wilder (8)	471
7.	Ridley Scott (5)	361
8.	Quentin Tarantino (7)	313
9.	Orson Welles (4)	306
10.	Akira Kurosawa (7)	301
11.	Charles Chaplin (6)	299
12.	Sergio Leone (3)	269
13.	Ingmar Bergman (8)	262
14.	James Cameron (5)	244

15.	David Lean (5)	238
16.	Federico Fellini (5)	237
17.	Roman Polanski (7)	230
18.	Howard Hawks (8)	227
19.	Victor Fleming (2)	217
20.	Jean-Luc Godard (8)	213
21.	John Ford (7)	213
22.	Fritz Lang (3)	210
23.	Joel and Ethan Coen (5)	202
24.	Michael Curtiz (4)	197
25.	Christopher Nolan (6)	188
26.	Frank Capra (5)	187
27.	Jean Renoir (4)	187
28.	John Huston (7)	176
29.	Woody Allen (6)	174
30.	George Lucas (5)	174
31.	François Truffaut (5)	164
32.	Milos Forman (3)	159
33.	David Fincher (3)	157
34.	Robert Zemeckis (3)	155
35.	Stanley Donen (2)	155
36.	Michelangelo Antonioni (6)	146
37.	Friedrich Wilhelm Murnau (3)	143
38.	Andrei Tarkovsky (5)	138
39.	George Cukor (8)	136
40.	Robert Altman (5)	135
41.	Robert Bresson (7)	132
42.	Carl Theodor Dreyer (4)	130
43.	David Lynch (5)	129
44.	Elia Kazan (4)	129
45.	Luis Buñuel (10)	128

46.	Peter Jackson (3)	128
47.	Yasujiro Ozu (2)	126
48.	Carol Reed (1)	121
49.	Rob Reiner (4)	117
50.	Clint Eastwood (6)	113
51.	Sam Peckinpah (4)	110
52.	Frank Darabont (2)	109
53.	Buster Keaton (2)	109
54.	Joseph L. Mankiewicz (3)	107
55.	Sidney Lumet (5)	105
56.	Sergei M. Eisenstein (3)	104
57.	William Wyler (6)	99
58.	Vittorio De Sica (2)	98
59.	Krzysztof Kieslowski (5)	94
60.	Andy and Lana Wachowski (1)	92
61.	Terry Jones (2)	91
62.	Jonathan Demme (3)	87
63.	Wong Kar-wai (2)	87
64.	Irvin Kershner (1)	84
65.	Satyajit Ray (3)	83
66.	Jean-Pierre Jeunet (2)	83
67.	Brian De Palma (5)	82
68.	Roberto Rossellini (3)	82
69.	Mike Nichols (5)	80
70.	Robert Wise (4)	80
71.	Jacques Tati (3)	80
72.	Ernst Lubitsch (5)	78
73.	Kenji Mizoguchi (3)	78
74.	Charles Laughton (1)	78
75.	Pedro Almodóvar (4)	77
76.	Hayao Miyazaki (3)	76

77.	D.W. Griffith (4)	74
78.	Terrence Malick (4)	74
79.	Marcel Carné (2)	72
80.	John Lasseter (2)	72
81.	Curtis Hanson (2)	71
82.	Ang Lee (4)	70
83.	Michael Cimino (1)	70
84.	George Roy Hill (3)	69
85.	William Friedkin (2)	69
86.	Bernardo Bertolucci (3)	68
87.	John McTiernan (2)	67
88.	Vincente Minnelli (5)	66
89.	Leo McCarey (4)	66
90.	Fernando Meirelles (1)	64
91.	Luc Besson (2)	63
92.	Darren Aronofsky (4)	62
93.	Michael Powell (4)	62
94.	Terry Gilliam (4)	61
95.	Wim Wenders (4)	61
96.	Max Ophüls (3)	60
97.	John Carpenter (5)	59
98.	Nicholas Ray (3)	59
99.	Jean Vigo (2)	59
100.	Danny Boyle (3)	58

Sources

Cinema Media
Cahiers du Cinéma (F): 100 Films, 2012.
Cinema (D): Die 100 besten Filme aller Zeiten, 2012.
Empire (UK): The 100 Greatest Movies of All Time, 2008.
empireonline.com (UK): Top 100 World Cinema, 2013.
imdb.com (USA): Top 100 Movies, 2013.
rottentomatoes.com (USA): Top 100 Movies of All Time, 2013.
Sight and Sound (UK): The Greatest Films Poll, 2012.
Sight and Sound (UK): Directors' Top 100, 2012.
Steadycam (D): 30 Lieblingsfilme, 2007.
Total Film (UK): 100 Greatest Movies of All Time, 2010.
Total Film (UK): Reader's Top 100 Movies of All Time, 2006.

Institutions
Alliance of Women Film Journalists (USA): Top 100 Films List, 2007.
American Film Institute (USA): Top 100 American Movies, 2007.
Bundeszentrale für politische Bildung (D): Der Filmkanon, 2003.
Toronto Film Festival (CAN): Essential 100, 2010.

Other Media
ABC TV (AUS): Top 100 Movies, 2011.
Bild (D): Die 30 besten Filme aller Zeiten, 2012.
Channel 4 (UK): 50 Films to See Before You Die, 2011.
Entertainment Weekly (USA): Top 50 Cult Movies, 2005.
Esquire (USA): The 75 Movies Every Man Should See, 2012.

GigaPedia.de (D): Top 100—Die besten Filme aller Zeiten, 2012.

HÖRZU (D): Die 100 besten Filme, 2011.

kabel eins (D): Top 100, 2004.

nerve.com (USA): Top 50 Cult Movies, 2011.

The Spectator (UK): 50 Essential Films, 2009.

Süddeutsche Zeitung (D): Cinemathek, 2005/2006.

Sydney Morning Herald (AUS): Top 100, 2003.

Time Magazine (USA): All-Time 100 Movies, 2011.

The Times (UK): Top 100, 2008.

TV Digital (D): Die besten Filme aller Zeiten, 2012.

TV Movie (D): Die 50 besten Filme der Welt, 2012.

Vanity Fair (USA): The 50 Greatest Films of All Times, 2005.

Die Zeit (D): 50 Klassiker, 2005/2006.

Critics' Lists

James Berardinelli (USA): Top 100, 2009.

Claudio Colombo (I): Classifica generale die migliori film di tutti i tempi, 2013.

Edward Copeland (USA): Top 100, 2012.

Tim Dirks (USA): Top 100, 2013.

Roger Ebert (USA): 100 Greatest Movies, 2003.

Jim Emerson (USA): 101 Movies You Must See Before ..., 2006.

Peter W. Jansen (D): Eine Geschichte des Kinos in 100 Filmen, 2003.

Glenn Kenny (USA): Top 100 Alternative List, 2007.

Bill Mousoulis (USA): Top 100, 2003.

Gail Kinn/Jim Piazza (USA): The Greatest Movies Ever, 2008.

Sources

Peter Rainer (USA): Top 129, 2005.
Paul Schrader (USA): The Canon, 2006.
Richard Thompson (USA): Top 100, 2007.

Websites

allocine.fr (F): Les 100 meilleurs films de tous les temps selon les spectateurs, 2013.
artsforge.com (USA): Best Films, 2005.
bestonly.com (USA): Top 100, 2005.
cineasten.de (D): Top 100, 2013.
cineclubdecaen.com (F): Top 100, 2012.
cinemagora.com (F): Meilleurs films de tous les temps, 2013.
cinemarati.org (USA): Top 100, 2006.
cinetrafic.fr (F): Les 100 meilleurs films Cinéma, 2013.
combustiblecelluloid.com (USA): Top 100, 2007.
coolmaterial.com (USA): Best Movies A-Z, 2013.
die100bestenfilme.de (D): Top 100, 2006.
digitaldreamdoor.com (USA): Top 100, 2006.
film.the-fan.net (D): Top 100, 2013.
filmcrave.com (USA): Top Movies of All Time, 2013.
filmfuchs.de (D): Top 100—All-Time Favorites, 2012.
films101.com (USA): The Best Movies of All Time, 2013.
foreignfilms.com (USA): Top 100, 2013.
icheckmovies.com (USA): Top 100, 2013.
lifed.com (USA): Top 100: Best Movies (of All-Time), 2012.
listsofbests.com (USA): The Cinematheque—Top 10 Project, 2008.
melhoresfilmes.com (BRA): 100 melhores filmes de todos os tempos, 2013.
moviecompound.com (USA): Top 100, 2004.

moviefanatic.com (USA): Top 100 Films of All Time, 2013.

phi-phenomenon.org (USA): Top 100 Films, 2012.

ranker.com (USA): The Best Movies of All Time, 2013.

roughoat.com (USA): Top 100, 2005.

shadowsonthewall.co.uk (UK): Top 100, 2004.

slantmagazine.com (USA): Essential 100, 2004.

thecityreview.com (USA): Top 100 Sound Films, 2005.

theessentialfilms.blogspot.de (D): The 100 Greatest Movies
   of All Time, 2011.

thelarrypage.com (USA): Top 100, 2005.

thependragon.co.uk (UK): 100 Greatest Films, 2013.

theyshootpictures.com (USA): Top 100, 2013.

topcinefilm.free.fr (F): 100 meilleurs films, 2013.

toptenreviews.com (USA): Best Movies of All Time, 2013.

tv.cream.org (UK): Top 100, 2003.

uneporte.net (F): Top 100, 2004.